하늬바람 지음

기분이
어때?

How do you feel ?

기분이 어때? How do you feel?

지은이	Written by	하늬바람 Hanuibaram

발행일	Date of publication	2022년 5월 10일 May 10th, 2022
펴낸곳	Published by	주식회사 부크크 BOOKK
출판사등록	Registration as a publisher	2014. 07. 15.(제2014-16호)
주 소	Adress	서울시 금천구 가산디지털1로 119 SK트윈타워 A동 305호
		A-305,119,Gasandigital 1,Geumcheon Seoul, Korea
전 화	Telephone	1670-8316
이메일	E-mail	info@bookk.co.kr

ISBN 979-11-372-8205-6

www.bookk.co.kr
Copyright© 하늬바람 2022

늘 고마워요 ♡

머 리 말

안녕하세요!

 요즘 K-culture로 인해 전 세계적으로 많은 한국어 학습자들이 생겨났고, 그 결과 많은 한국어 학습 교재들이 출판되었습니다.
다만 대부분 단계별로 출판되는 통합 교재이다 보니 한국어 학습자들은 이를 통해 다양한 감정을 표현하는 기분 표현을 배울 수 없습니다. 게다가 한국어에는 다양한 감정이 섞인 표현이 많아 다른 언어로 완벽하게 번역하기가 어렵습니다.

 이 책은 행복, 분노, 놀라움, 두려움, 슬픔의 감정으로 표현할 수 있는 100가지 기분 표현을 정리했습니다. 또한 실제 생활에서 경험할 수 있는 상황들을 설명해 주기 때문에 그 표현들을 쉽게 이해할 수 있습니다. 이는 학습자들이 어떤 상황에서 어떤 표현을 사용해야 하는지 이해하기 쉽도록 하기 위해서입니다.

 이 책이 당신의 기분을 한국어로 적절하게 잘 표현하는 데 도움이 될 것이라고 확신합니다.

Introduction

Hello, Everyone!

 These days, K-culture has created many Korean learners around the world, and as a result, many Korean learning textbooks have been published.

However, since most of them are integrated textbooks published step by step, Korean learners cannot learn various feeling expressions through them.

Besides, there are many expressions mixed with diverse emotions in Korean, making it difficult to translate them into other languages.

 This book summarizes 100 expressions of feelings that can be expressed in emotions of happiness, anger, surprise, fear, and sadness. It also explains situations that can be experienced in real life so that you can easily understand those expressions.

The purpose of this is to make it easier to understand which expression to use in which situation. And this book is written by using a colloquial expression.

 I guarantee that this book will help you express your feelings adequately in Korean.

How to use this book

기분 표현의 기본형과 발음기호:
QR 코드를 스캔하면 국립국어원 한국어-영어 학습사전 사이트로 연결되어
발음을 들을 수 있습니다.
The basic form of feeling expression and pronunciation symbols:
If you scan the QR, you can hear the pronunciation by connecting to
the Korean-English Learner's Dictionary of the National Institute of
Korean Language.

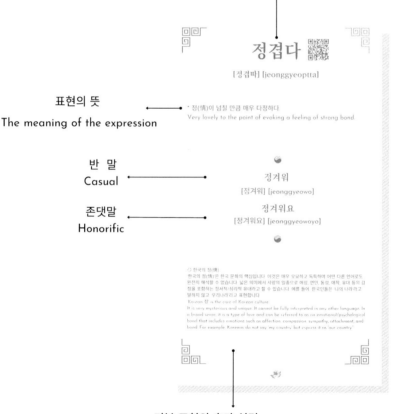

정겹다

[정겹따] [jeonggyeoptta]

표현의 뜻
The meaning of the expression

" 정(情)이 넘칠 만큼 매우 다정하다
Very lovely to the point of evoking a feeling of strong bond.

반 말
Casual

정거워
[정거워] [jeonggyeowo]

존댓말
Honorific

정거워요
[정거워요] [jeonggyeowoyo]

① 한국의 정(情)
한국의 정(情)은 한국 문화의 핵심입니다. 이것은 매우 오묘하고 독특하여 어떤 다른 언어로도
완전히 해석할 수 없습니다. 넓은 의미에서 사랑의 일종으로 애정, 연민, 동정, 애착, 유대 등의 감
정을 포함하는 정서적·심리적 유대라고 할 수 있습니다. 예를 들어 한국인들은 나의 나라라고
말하지 않고 우리나라라고 표현합니다.
Korean 정 is the core of Korean culture.
It is very mysterious and unique. It cannot be fully interpreted in any other language. In
a broad sense, it is a type of love and can be referred to as an emotional/psychological
bond that includes emotions such as affection, compassion, sympathy, attachment, and
bond. For example, Koreans do not say 'my country' but express it as 'our country'.

기분 표현의 추가 설명
Additional explanation of feelings

오른쪽 페이지는 기분 표현을 사용할 수 있는 상황을 설명합니다.

The right page explains the situations in which feeling expressions can be used.

우리 아버지께선 할머니께 안마를 해드리고, 담소를 나누셨어요.
My father gave his grandmother a massage and chatted with her.
"정겨워요"

설 연휴에는 온 가족이 모여서 잔치를 해.
Every Seollal holiday, my whole family gets together and has a feast.
"정겨워"

한 노부부가 서로를 보듬으며 손을 잡고 걷고 있어요.
An old couple is walking hand in hand, caring for each other.
"정겨워요"

우리 어머니께선 맛있는 김밥을 만들어 모든 이웃집에 나눠주셨어요.
My mother made delicious Gimbap and shared it with all her neighbors.
"정겨워요"

오랜만에 시골 장터에 갔어. 예전 그대로네.
It's been a while since I went to a countryside market. It's the same as it ever was.
"정겨워"

* 표시가 되어 있는 부분은 '『국립국어원 한국어-영어 학습사전』 (https://krdict.korean.go.kr/eng)'에서 발췌한 내용으로 저작권은 국립국어원에 있습니다.

The part marked with * is an excerpt from the Korean-English Learners' Dictionary of the National Institute of Korean Language (https://krdict.korean.go.kr/eng), and the copyright belongs to the National Institute of Korean Language.

행복 / HAPPINESS

TABLE OF CONTENTS

분노 / ANGER

놀라움 / SURPRISE

두려움 / FEAR

슬픔 / SADNESS

행복

HAPPINESS

정겹다

[정겹따] [jeonggyeoptta]

* 정(情)이 넘칠 만큼 매우 다정하다.

Very lovely to the point of evoking a feeling of strong bond.

정겨워

[정겨워] [jeonggyeowo]

정겨워요

[정겨워요] [jeonggyeowoyo]

◎ 한국의 정(情)

'한국의 정(情)'은 한국 문화의 핵심입니다. 이것은 매우 오묘하고 독특하며 어떤 다른 언어로도 완전히 해석할 수 없습니다. 넓은 의미에서 사랑의 일종으로 애정, 연민, 동정, 애착, 유대 등의 감정을 포함하는 정서적/심리적 유대라고 할 수 있습니다.

예를 들어, 한국인들은 '나의 나라'라고 말하지 않고 '우리나라'라고 표현합니다.

'Korean 정' is the core of Korean culture.

It is very mysterious and unique. It cannot be fully interpreted in any other language. In a broad sense, it is a type of love and can be referred to as an emotional/psychological bond that includes emotions such as affection, compassion, sympathy, attachment, and bond.

For example, Koreans do not say 'my country' but express it as 'our country.'

우리 아버지께선 할머니께 안마를 해드리고,
담소를 나누셨어요.
My father gave his grandmother a
massage and chatted with her.
"정겨워요"

설 연휴에는 온 가족이 모여서 잔치를 해.
Every Seollal holiday, my whole family
gets together and has a feast.
"정겨워"

한 노부부가 서로를 보듬으며 손을 잡고
걷고 있어요.
An old couple is walking hand in hand,
caring for each other.
"정겨워요"

우리 어머니께선 맛있는 김밥을 만들어
모든 이웃집에 나눠주셨어요.
My mother made delicious Gimbap and
shared it with all her neighbors.
"정겨워요"

오랜만에 시골 장터에 갔어. 예전 그대로네.
It's been a while since I went to a
countryside market.
It's the same as it ever was.
"정겨워"

다정하다

[다정하다] [dajeonghada]

* 마음이 따뜻하고 정(情)이 많다.
Warm-hearted and affectionate.

●

다정해

[다정해] [dajeonghae]

다정해요

[다정해요] [dajeonghaeyo]

●

내 친구는 항상 다른 사람들을 잘 챙겨.
My friend always takes good care of
other people.

"다정해"

내 남자친구는 내가 비를 맞지 않게 내 쪽으로
우산을 기울여 씌워줘.
My boyfriend tilts his umbrella to my side
so that I don't get rained on.

"다정해"

내 생일을 기억하고 카드 보내줘서 고마워요.
It was thoughtful of you to remember
my birthday and send me a card.

"다정해요"

한국 사람들은 아주 친절하고 상냥해.
한국 여행을 갔을 때 한국 사람들은 자신의
일이 아닌데도 열정적으로 날 도와주었어.
Koreans are very friendly and hospitable.
When I went on a trip to Korea, they
enthusiastically helped me even though
it didn't concern them directly.

"다정해"

우리 아빠는 사려 깊고 따뜻하고 아주 친절해요.
My dad is thoughtful, warm, and extremely
kind.

"다정해요"

사랑스럽다

[사랑스럽따] [sarangseureoptta]

* 사랑을 느낄 만큼 귀엽다.

So cute as to evoke a feeling of affection.

●

사랑스러워

[사랑스러워] [sarangseureowo]

사랑스러워요

[사랑스러워요] [sarangseureowoyo]

●

◎ -스럽다 [쓰럽따] [seureoptta]

명사 뒤에 붙어 '그러한 성질이 있음'의 뜻을 더하고 형용사로 만드는 단어.

This word is attached after a noun and adds the meaning of 'having such attributes' so that the noun becomes an adjective.

그 아기는 깨물어 주고 싶을 만큼 귀여워.

The baby is so cute that I want to bite him.

"사랑스러워"

나에게 웃으며 걸어오는 내 여자친구를
안아주고 싶어.

I want to hug my girlfriend as she walks
toward me with a smile.

"사랑스러워"

우리 아들의 어린 시절 사진을 보고 있어요.
너무 귀엽고 예뻐요.

I'm looking at my son's childhood pictures.
He's so adorable and lovely.

"사랑스러워요"

환하게 웃는 아이들과 아내를 보니 너무 행복해.
항상 내 곁에 있는 아내와 아이들을 보면 사랑이
느껴져요.

I'm so happy to see my wife and kids smiling
brightly. When I see my wife and kids who
are always by my side, I feel love.

"사랑스러워요"

우리 아기가 너무 귀여워서 마구마구 뽀뽀해 줬어.

My baby is so cute that I lavished kisses
upon him.

"사랑스러워"

설레다

[설레다] [seolleda]

* 마음이 차분하지 않고 들떠서 두근거리다.

For one's heart not to be calm but to flutter because one is excited.

●

설레

[설레] [seolle]

설레요

[설레요] [seolleyo]

●

개를 보자 심장이 두근거렸어.

My heart fluttered when I saw him.

"설레"

난 겨우내 봄을 기다렸어요.

날씨가 점점 따뜻해지고 해가 길어지고 있어요.

I've been waiting for spring all winter.

It's getting warmer and the days are

getting longer.

"설레요"

우린 내일 한국으로 휴가를 갈 거예요.

We are going on vacation to Korea tomorrow.

"설레요"

이번 주말에 하준이와 데이트가 있어서

주말이 너무 기다려져.

I have a date with Hajun this weekend,

so I'm looking forward to this weekend.

"설레"

전 세계 어린이들은 산타 할아버지를 기다리고 있어.

Children all over the world are waiting for

Santa Claus.

"설레"

내일 난생처음으로 운전면허증을 받을 거예요.

I'm going to get my driver's license tomorrow

for the first time in my life.

"설레요"

보고 싶다

[보고십따] [bogosiptta]

보다 + 싶다 = 보고 싶다

그리워하는 마음을 갖고 있다.

This means that one misses someone or something.

보고 싶어

[보고시퍼] [bogosipeo]

보고 싶어요

[보고시퍼요] [bogosipeoyo]

◎ 보다 [보다] [boda]

* 사람을 만나다. 눈으로 대상의 존재나 겉모습을 알다.

To meet a person. To perceive with eyes the existence or appearance of an object.

◎ 싶다 [십따] [siptta]

* 앞의 말이 나타내는 내용을 하고자 하는 의도나 욕구가 있음을 나타내는 말.

An auxiliary adjective used to indicate that the speaker has an intention or desire to do what the preceding statement describes.

오늘은 유학 간 아들 생일이라서 자꾸 아들이
생각나.
Today is the birthday of my son who
went abroad to study, so I can't stop
thinking about him.
"보고 싶어"

몇 년 동안 편지를 주고받은 펜팔 친구가 있는데,
올해는 걔를 꼭 직접 만났으면 좋겠어.
I have a pen pal whom I exchanged letters
with for years. I really hope to meet her
in person this year.
"보고 싶어"

요즘 그 도시가 힙 하대. 그래서 이번 휴가 때
그 도시로 여행을 갈 수 있었으면 좋겠어.
I've heard a lot about the city being hip
these days.
So I hope I can travel to the city during
this vacation.
"(그 도시가 어떤지) 보고 싶어"

오늘 외국에 사는 삼촌이 우리 집에 놀러 오세요.
그래서 아침부터 우리 아이들은 삼촌을 애타게
기다리고 있어요.
My uncle who lives abroad is visiting my house
today. So since this morning, my kids have been
anxiously waiting for him to arrive soon.
"보고 싶어요"

그립다

[그립따] [geuriptta]

* 1. 매우 보고 싶고 만나고 싶다.

Wanting to see and meet someone very much.

* 2. 어떤 것이 매우 필요하거나 없어서 아쉽다.

Feeling the lack of something because one needs it desperately or does not have it.

그리워

[그리워] [geuriwo]

그리워요

[그리워요] [geuriwoyo]

◎ 보고 싶다 vs 그립다

· 보고 싶다 : 주로 (다른 사람이나 장소가) 쉽게 만나거나 볼 수 있을 때 사용한다.

This word is mostly used when it is easy to meet or see someone or something.

· 그립다 : 주로 (다른 사람이나 장소가) 만나거나 보기 어렵거나 더 이상 만나거나 볼 수 없을 때 사용한다.

This word is mostly used when it is difficult to meet or see someone or something.

우리 할머니께서는 2년 전에 돌아가셨어요.

My grandmother passed away 2 years ago.

"그리워요"

그곳은 내 어린 시절의 추억을 떠오르게 했어요.

The place summoned up memories of my
childhood.

"그리워요"

우린 전국 방방곡곡을 여행했어.
정말 잊지 못할 즐거운 시간들이었어.

We traveled all over the country.
It was an unforgettable and enjoyable time.

"그리워"

마스크를 쓰지 않아도 되던 시절로 돌아가고 싶어.

I want to go back to the days when I didn't
have to wear a mask.

"그리워"

옛날로 다시 돌아가서 어릴 적 친구들과 놀고 싶어.

I would like to go back into the past and
hang out with my childhood friends again.

"그리워"

살인적인 폭염이야, 그치? 겨울 날씨가 그리워!

This is a killing heat wave, isn't it?
I miss the winter weather!

"그리워"

애틋하다

[애트타다] [aeteutada]

* 1. 섭섭하고 안타까워 애가 타는 듯하다.
One's heart going to someone or something out of regret
or sympathy.
* 2. 아끼고 위하는 정이 깊다.
Having deep affection and love for someone.

●

애틋해

[애트태] [aeteutae]

애틋해요

[애트태요] [aeteutaeyo]

●

내 남자친구는 서울 출장 중인데 벌써 보고 싶어!
My boyfriend is on a business trip in Seoul.
I miss him already!

"애틋해"

학기 중에 부모님을 자주 찾아뵙지 못해서
부모님이 너무 보고 싶어요.
I haven't visited my parents often during
the semester, so I really miss them.

"애틋해요"

그들은 10년간의 결혼 생활 후 헤어졌어요.
그는 아쉽고 애석하게 그 시절을 되돌아봤어요.
They bust up after ten years of marriage.
He looked back to those days fondly and
wistfully.

"애틋해요"

로미오와 줄리엣의 사랑은 결국 이루어지지 않아.
Romeo and Juliet's love doesn't come true
eventually.

"애틋해"

다른 가족들과 멀리 떨어져 사시는 할머니를
자주 보러 가지 못했어요.
할머니와 전화 통화를 할 때 드는 마음.
I couldn't go often to see my grandmother
who lived far away from other families.
This is how I feel when I talk to her on the
phone.

"애틋해요"

훈훈하다

[훈훈하다] [hunhunhada]

* 마음을 부드럽게 녹여 주는 따뜻함이 있다.

Having warmth that softens the heart.

●

훈훈해

[훈훈해] [hunhunhae]

훈훈해요

[훈훈해요] [hunhunhaeyo]

●

너희 둘이 끈끈한 우정을 쌓아 가는
모습을 보니 마음이 따뜻해져.
It's heartwarming to see two form
a strong friendship.

"훈훈해"

그 카페에서 일하는 남자는 너무 잘생겼어!
The guy who works at the cafe is
very good-looking.

"훈훈해"

우리 어머니와 이웃들은 김치를 불우한 이웃과
나누었어요.
My mother and her neighbors shared
the kimchi with less fortunate neighbors.

"훈훈해요"

걔의 친절한 말에 마음이 따뜻해졌어.
My heart was warmed by her kind words.

"훈훈해"

우린 서로 격려하고 의지했어.
We encouraged and depend on each other.

"훈훈해"

학생들이 어르신께 자리를 양보하는 모습은
언제나 보기 좋아요.
Students who offer their seats
to elderly people always look good.

"훈훈해요"

흐뭇하다

[흐무타다] [heumutada]

* 마음에 들어 매우 만족스럽다.
Being very happy and pleased with something.

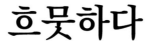

흐뭇해

[흐무태] [heumutae]

흐뭇해요

[흐무태요] [heumutaeyo]

몇 년 동안 열심히 노력해서,
마침내 내 집을 갖게 됐어.
After working hard for years,
I finally got my own house.

"흐뭇해"

우리 부모님께선 제가 만든 음식을 너무
좋아하세요.
My parents love the food which I make.

"흐뭇해요"

매번 네 도움만 받았는데, 이제 내가 도울 수
있어서 너무 기뻐.
I've only received your help every time,
but I'm so happy that I can help you now.

"흐뭇해"

우리 아이들이 정원에서 즐겁게 놀고 있어.
아이들이 밝고 건강하게 커가는 모습을 볼 때
드는 마음.
My kids are having fun in my garden.
This is how I feel when I see them growing
up bright and healthy.

"흐뭇해"

여가 시간에 가야금을 연주하는 것을 좋아해.
다른 사람들이 내가 가야금 연주를 잘한다고
말해줄 때 드는 마음.
I like to play the gayageum in my free
time. This is how I feel when others say
I'm good at playing the gayageum.

"흐뭇해요"

든든하다

[든든하다] [deundeunhada]

* 어떤 것에 대한 믿음이 있어 마음이 힘차다.
Feeling reassured thanks to faith in something.

든든해

[든든해] [deundeunhae]

든든해요

[든든해요] [deundeunhaeyo]

냉장고에 음식이 많으니 왠지 안정감이 들어.
With so much food in the fridge,
I somehow feel secure.
"든든해"

우리 아버지께서는 제가 계속 버틸 수 있게
힘을 주세요.
My father give me strength to carry on.
"든든해요"

우리 어머니께서 돌아가셨을 때 갠 정말
든든한 버팀목이 되어 주었어.
When my mother passed away,
he was a real support.
"든든해"

성원이는 내가 힘들 때 언제나 내 곁에 있어
주었어.
Seongwon was always there for me
during the difficulties I faced.
"든든해"

난 밤에 혼자 집에 걸어가는 게 무서워.
그래서 내 남자친구가 항상 집까지 바래다줘.
I'm frightened of walking home alone
in the dark.
So my boyfriend always walks me home.
"든든해"

행복하다

[행보카다] [haengbokada]

* 삶에서 충분한 만족과 기쁨을 느껴 흐뭇하다.
Being delighted as one feels enough satisfaction
or enjoyment in life.

●

행복해

[행보캐] [haengbokae]

행복해요

[행보캐요] [haengbokaeyo]

●

난 지금 제주도에서 여름휴가를 즐기고 있어.

I'm enjoying my summer vacation in Jeju
Island now.

"행복해"

우리 아들과 딸이 즐겁게 놀고 있어요.
집안에 아이들의 웃음소리가 가득해요.

My son and daughter are making merry.
My house rang with children's laughter.

"행복해요"

난 의지할 수 있는 진정한 친구가 몇 명 있어.

I have a few true friends that I can count
on.

"행복해"

우린 정말 즐거운 시간을 보냈고, 오늘 밤 너와
함께 있어서 너무 좋아.

We've had a lovely time and It's so good
to be here with you tonight.

"행복해"

우린 결혼식을 계획한 후 몇 달 동안 이 순간을
기다려왔어. 오늘이 바로 그날이야!

We'd been looking forward to this moment
for months after planning our wedding day.
Today is the day!

"행복해요"

고맙다

[고ː맙따] [goːmaptta]

* 남이 자신을 위해 무엇을 해주어서 마음이 흐뭇하고 보답하고 싶다.

Pleased and wanting to return a favor to someone.

●

고마워

[고마워] [goːmawo]

고마워요

[고마워요] [goːmawoyo]

●

오늘 밤에 이렇게 와줘서 참 기뻐.
I'm so glad you could make it tonight.

"고마워"

우리 부모님께선 저에게 항상 모든 것을
아낌없이 주세요.
My parents always give me everything
generously.

"고마워요"

내가 실직했을 때 내 가장 친한 친구가
큰 힘이 되어 주었어.
My best friend was so supportive when
I lost my job.

"고마워"

난 여행 중이라 큰 가방을 들고 있었어.
지하철역에 엘리베이터가 없어서 계단으로
가방을 옮겨야 했어.
그런데 누군가가 매우 친절하게 도와줬어.
I was carrying a big bag because I was
traveling. There was no elevator at the
subway station, so I had to carry my bag
by the stairs.
But someone helped me very kindly.

"고마워요"

깜빡하고 노트북을 놓고 왔는데 동료가 챙겨줬어.
I forgot and left my laptop, but my colleague
brought it for me.

"고마워"

자랑스럽다

[자랑스럽따] [jarangseureoptta]

* 자랑할 만한 데가 있다.
Having something to be boastful of.

자랑스러워

[자랑스러워] [jarangseureowo]

자랑스러워요

[자랑스러워요] [jarangseureowoyo]

◎ -스럽다 [쓰럽따] [seureoptta]
명사 뒤에 붙어 '그러한 성질이 있음'의 뜻을 더하고 형용사로 만드는 단어.
This word is attached after a noun and adds the meaning of 'having such attributes' so that the noun becomes an adjective.

김연아는 올림픽에서 메달을 딴 최초의 한국인
피겨 스케이팅 선수예요.

Yuna Kim was the first Korean figure skater
to win a medal at the Olympics.

"자랑스러워요"

요즘 한국 문화는 외국인 친구들에게 인기가
많아서 외국인 친구들에게 한국 문화를 소개할
때마다 내가 한국인인 것이 너무 기분이 좋아요.

These days, Korean culture is popular with
foreign friends, so it feels great to be a
Korean whenever I introduce K-culture to
my foreign friends.

"자랑스러워"

우리 딸은 조기졸업을 앞두고 있고,
졸업식 때 상을 받을 거예요.

My daughter has early graduation ahead,
and she'll be given a prize at the graduation
ceremony.

"자랑스러워"

내 스스로도 믿기지 않을 만큼 완벽한 연주를 했어.
I played a perfect performance that even I
found incredible.

"자랑스러워"

우리 아내는 회사에서 항상 최선을 다해요.
그녀는 이번에 최연소 경영진으로 승진했어요.
My wife always does her best at work. This time,
she was promoted to the youngest manager.

"자랑스러워요"

뿌듯하다

[뿌드타다] [ppudeutada]

* 기쁨이나 감격이 마음에 가득하다.
Fully joyful or moved.

●

뿌듯해

[뿌드태] [ppudeutae]

뿌듯해요

[뿌드태요] [ppudeutaeyo]

●

우리 아이가 처음 학교에 가는 날이에요.

It's my kid's first day at school.

"뿌듯해요"

일을 시작하고, 난 빠르게 승진했어.

After I started working at the company,

I moved up quickly.

"뿌듯해"

우리 동생은 어려운 시험을 한 번에 합격했어.

My brother passed the difficult test at once.

"뿌듯해"

몇 주 동안 밤새워 일했고,

마침내 모든 디자인을 완성했어.

I've been working all night for weeks,

and I've finally completed all the designs.

"뿌듯해"

이번 계약은 어려웠지만 결국 또 따냈어요.

이번 건을 성공적으로 끝내서 정말 기뻐요.

This contract was challenging, but I ended

up closing it again. I am extremely pleased

that I wrapped it up in success.

"뿌듯해요"

열심히 키운 꽃이 만발한 정원을 볼 때 드는 마음.

This is how I feel when I look at the garden

where the flowers that I worked hard to grow

are in full bloom.

"뿌듯해"

벅차다

[벅차다] [beokchada]

* 1. 어떤 일을 해내거나 견디기가 어렵다.
Difficult to do or endure something.
* 2. 기쁘거나 희망에 차서 가슴이 뿌듯하다.
One's heart being filled with joy or hope.

●

벅차

[벅차] [beokcha]

벅차요

[벅차요] [beokchayo]

●

◎ 벅차다 vs 버겁다
'벅차다'는 긍정적이거나 부정적인 감정에 사용한다.
Use '벅차다' for negative or positive emotions.
'버겁다'는 부정적인 감정을 표현할 때만 사용한다.
Use '버겁다' only for negative emotions.

나 혼자 처리해야 할 일이 산더미야.
I have so many things I have to handle
on my own.

"벅차"

그게 불가능하다고 말하는 건 아니지만,
잘 하는 건 엄청나게 어려울 거야.
I am not saying it couldn't be done,
but it would be extremely difficult
to do it well.

"벅차"

서울 축제는 기쁨, 음악, 춤, 웃음, 그리고
재미가 흘러넘치는 시간이에요.
The Seoul festival is an exuberant time
of joy, music, dancing, laughter, and fun.

"벅차요"

몇 년 동안 모아둔 돈으로 꿈에 그리던 차를 샀어.
I bought my dream car with the money I had
earned and saved for several years.

"벅차"

종종 말썽을 부리던 아들의 고등학교 졸업식이 내일
있어요. 아들이 무사히 졸업한다니 감개무량해요.
Tomorrow is the high-school graduation
ceremony for my son who often caused trouble.
I'm full of emotions at the fact that he is
 graduating soundly.

"벅차요"

뭉클하다

[뭉클하다] [mungkeulhada]

* 어떤 감정이나 느낌이 매우 강하게 마음에 생겨 가슴에 꽉 차는 느낌.

Feeling that one's heart is filled with a strong emotion or sentiment.

뭉클해

[뭉클해] [mungkeulhae]

뭉클해요

[뭉클해요] [mungkeunghayo]

2002 월드컵은 한국인들이 하나로 어우러지는
행사였어. 그때 생각만 하면 가슴이 울컥해.
The 2002 World Cup was an event that
brought harmony and unity to Koreans.
Every time I think of it I get emotional.
"뭉클해요"

한국의 한센병 환자들을 위해 평생을 바친
오스트리아 수녀님들의 이야기를 들었어요.
I heard stories of Austrian nuns who devoted
their lives to leprosy patients in Korea.
"뭉클해요"

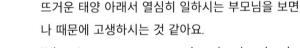

그 바이올리니스트는 연주 도중 현이 끊어졌음에도
불구하고 관객들에게 아름다운 연주를 들려주기
위해 최선을 다했어요.
Even though a string was cut off during the
performance, the violinist did his best to present
a beautiful performance to the audience.
"뭉클해"

뜨거운 태양 아래서 열심히 일하시는 부모님을 보면
나 때문에 고생하시는 것 같아요.
When I see my parents working hard under the
hot sun, I feel like they're struggling for my sake.
"뭉클해요"

가난하고 배고픈 그 아이는 부실한 도시락을 받아도
불평은커녕 감사의 쪽지를 잊지 않았어요.
Although the poor and hungry child was given
an inadequate lunch box, he didn't forget to
give a note of appreciation, let alone complain.
"뭉클해요"

감동하다

[감ː동하다] [gamːdonghada]

* 강하게 느껴 마음이 움직이다.
To be touched by something very deeply.

●

감동했어

[감ː동해써] [gam:donghaesseo]

감동했어요

[감ː동해써요] [gam:donghaesseoyo]

●

내 친구들은 내 생일에 깜짝파티를 해줬어.
My friends threw a surprise party
for my birthday.

"감동했어"

그 예술가는 팔과 손이 없이 태어났지만,
발로 아름다운 그림을 그릴 수 있어요.
The artist was born without arms and hands,
but he can paint beautiful pictures with his
feet.

"감동했어요"

난 그의 헌신과 추진력에 깊은 인상을 받았어.
I was impressed by his commitment and
drive.

"감동했어"

8살 난 우리 아들이 모아둔 용돈으로 내 생일
선물을 샀어.
My 8-year-old son bought my birthday
present with the little pocket money
that he had saved.

"감동했어"

어려운 환경 속에서도 최선을 다한 그의 모습은
많은 사람들에게 교훈을 줬어요.
Doing his best even in a difficult environment
taught many people a lesson.

"감동했어요"

감격스럽다

[감ː격쓰럽따] [gamːgyeoksseureoptta]

* 마음에 느끼는 감동이 크다.

Feeling or being touched by something very deeply.

●

감격스러워

[감ː격쓰러워] [gamːgyeoksseureowo]

감격스러워요

[감ː격쓰러워요] [gamːgyeoksseureowoyo]

●

◎ -스럽다 [쓰럽따] [seureoptta]

명사 뒤에 붙어 '그러한 성질이 있음'의 뜻을 더하고, 형용사로 만드는 단어.

This word is attached after a noun and adds the meaning of 'having such attributes' so that the noun becomes an adjective.

흠잡을 데 없는 4분간의 완벽한 연기가 끝나자
김연아 선수는 눈물을 흘렸어요.
When the flawless, four-minute performance
was over, Yuna Kim shed tears.
"감격스러워요"

우린 5년 넘게 임신하려고 노력해왔어.
오늘 아침에 임신 테스트기에 두 줄이 나왔어!
엄마가 된다니 너무 행복해!
We've been trying to get pregnant for over
5 years. My pregnancy test was positive this
morning! I'm so happy I'm going to be a mom!
"감격스러워"

고향에 30년 만에 돌아왔어요. 가슴이 벅차올라요.
I returned to my hometown after 30 years.
I'm overwhelmed.
"감격스러워요"

10년 동안 그토록 찾아 헤매던 어머니를 만난
그녀는 말로 표현할 수 없는 감동을 느꼈어.
Meeting her mother, for whom she had
searched desperately for 10 years, she felt
touched that she couldn't even say anything.
"감격스러워"

그 선수는 부상을 극복하고 마침내 우승을 차지했어.
The player overcame the injury and finally won
the championship.
"감격스러워"

후련하다

[후련하다] [huryeonhada]

* 마음에 답답하게 맺혔던 것이 풀려 시원하다.

Feeling light and relieved because one's anxiety has been resolved.

●

후련해

[후련해] [huryeonhae]

후련해요

[후련해요] [huryeonhaeyo]

●

학자금 대출을 갚고 나니 마음이 가벼워요.
The load is off my mind now that I
have cleared off my student loans.

"후련해요"

실컷 울고 나니 기분이 한결 나아졌어요.
I feel much better now that I've had a
good cry.

"후련해요"

밀린 과제를 모두 제출하고 나니 이제야
마음이 놓여.
Now that I've submitted all my
overdue assignments. I'm relieved.

"후련해"

너한테 쌓인 감정이 많았었어. 하고 싶은 말을
모두 털어놓고 나니 속이 시원해.
I had a lot of harbored feelings toward you.
I've said what I wanted to say, and now I
feel like a load's been taken off my chest.

"후련해"

친구랑 싸우고 한 달 동안 말을 하지 않아서 내내
마음이 불편했는데 화해하고 나니 마음이 놓였어.
I quarreled with my friend and didn't talk for
a month. I was uncomfortable the whole time,
but after we reconciled, I felt relieved.

"후련해"

개운하다

[개운하다] [gaeunhada]

* 기분이나 몸이 상쾌하고 가볍다.

One's mind or body feeling refreshed and light.

●

개운해

[개운해] [gaeunhae]

개운해요

[개운해요] [gaeunhaeyo]

●

입안이 텁텁해서 양치질을 했어요.

My mouth does not feel fresh at all.

So I brushed my teeth.

"개운해요"

며칠 동안 야근을 해서 피곤했어요.

푹 자고 일어났더니 이제 몸이 가벼워졌어요.

I was tired because I worked overtime for

a few days. I woke up after a good sleep,

so I feel lighter now.

"개운해요"

드디어 기말고사가 끝나서 친구들과 놀고 있어!

At last, my final exams are over!

So I'm hanging out with my friends!

"(마음이) 개운해"

머리를 식히기 위해 산책을 갔어.

산책을 다녀오니 정신이 맑아져서 날아갈 것 같아.

I went for a walk to cool off.

After taking a walk, my mind is so clear

that I could fly now.

"개운해"

땀 흘리며 운동하고 나니 기분이 상쾌해.

After working up a big sweat, I feel refreshed.

"개운해"

편안하다

[편안하다] [pyeonanhada]

* 몸이나 마음이 편하고 좋다.
One's body or mind being relaxed and good.

●

편안해

[편안해] [pyeonanhae]

편안해요

[편안해요] [pyeonanhaeyo]

●

난 긴 여행을 했어. 와~ 집에 오니 너무 좋다!

I had a long trip. oh~ It's nice to be home!

"편안해"

해변에 누워 선탠도 하고 차가운 음료도
홀짝거리고 있어요.

I'm lying on a beach, getting a tan and
sipping cold drinks.

"편안해요"

부드러운 마우스 패드는 마우스를 오래 사용해도
손목이 아프지 않아요. 오늘 하루 종일 일했는데
손목이 잘 받쳐져서 좋네요.

The soft mouse pad doesn't hurt my wrist
even after using the mouse for a long time.
I worked all day today, so it's nice to have
your wrist well-supported.

"편안해요"

하루 종일 불편한 옷을 입고 하이힐을 신고 있었어.
집에 오자마자 하이힐을 벗고 잠옷으로 갈아입었어.

I was wearing uncomfortable clothes and high
heels all day long. I took off my high heels
and got changed into pajamas the second I
get home.

"편안해"

지난 몇 주간 할 일이 산더미였어.
여유로운 일요일 소파에 누워 넷플릭스를 보고 있어.

I've had a lot on my plate in the last few weeks.
On this relaxing Sunday, I'm lying on the sofa
and watching Netflix.

"편안해"

황홀하다

[황홀하다] [hwangholhada]

* 1. 눈이 부셔 흐릿하게 보일 정도로 아름답고 화려하다.

Looking dazzlingly beautiful and splendid.

* 2. 마음이나 시선을 빼앗겨 흥분된 상태이다.

Being excited by something catching the eye or stealing the heart.

●

황홀해

[황홀해] [hwangholhae]

황홀해요

[황홀해요] [hwangholhaeyo]

●

난 성당의 고풍스러운 양식에 매료되었어.
I was fascinated by the archaic style
of the cathedral.
"황홀해"

걔가 내 청혼을 받아들였을 때 세상을 다
가진 기분이었어!
I was on top of the world when she
accepted my proposal of marriage.
"황홀해"

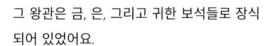

저녁의 일몰은 숨이 막힐 정도로 아름다웠어.
이렇게 아름다운 일몰은 본 적이 없어.
The sunset of the evening was
breathtaking. I've never seen such a
beautiful sunset before.
"황홀해"

그 왕관은 금, 은, 그리고 귀한 보석들로 장식
되어 있었어요.
The crown was blazed with ornaments of
gold, silver, and precious stones.
"황홀해요"

지금 팔로워 수가 220만 명이 넘었어요!
Now I have more than 2.2 million followers!
"황홀해요"

괜찮다

[괜찬타] [gwaenchanta]

* 별 문제가 없다.

Having no particular problems.

●

괜찮아

[괜차나] [gwaenchana]

괜찮아요

[괜차나요] [gwaenchanayo]

●

◎ 괜찮다

This means that something is better than I expected. It doesn't mean that it's really good or awesome or wonderful.

Also, you can use this when you don't want to receive other people's requests, suggestions, or gifts.

This is a softer expression than "싫어요(no)."

우린 두 번 실패했지만, 내년에 다시 도전하면 돼.

We had failed twice,

but we can try again next year.

"괜찮아"

가: 우리 오늘 밤에 필요한 거 다 준비됐어?

　 내가 가서 뭐 사 올까?

나: 응, 다 있어. 걱정 마.

A: Are we all sorted for tonight?

　 Do you need me to go buy anything?

B: Yeah, we are all sorted. Don't worry.

"괜찮아"

가: 새 제안서에 대해 어떻게 생각하세요?

나: 그렇게 좋은 건 아니고 괜찮은 정도네요.

A: What do you think about their new proposal?

B: Not bad. Decent.

"괜찮아요"

우리 아들이 나무에서 내려오다가 무릎이 까졌어.

My son skinned his knees climbing down the tree.

"괜찮아"

가: 나 아메리카노 주문하지 않았어?

나: 앗, 내 실수. 캐러멜마키아토 마시고 싶은 줄 알았어.

가: 아, 괜찮아! 어차피 둘 다 좋아해.

A: Didn't I order an americano?

B: Oop, my bad. I thought you wanted a caramel

macchiato.

A: Ah, no worries at all! I love them both anyway.

"괜찮아"

다행

[다행] [dahaeng]

다행 + 이다 = 다행이다 [다행이다] [dahaengida]

* 뜻밖에 운이 좋음.

A state of being lucky beyond expectation.

●

다행이야

[다행이야] [dahaengiya]

다행이에요

[다행이에요] [dahaengieyo]

●

◎ -이다 [이다] [ida]

주어가 지시하는 대상의 속성이나 부류를 지정하는 뜻을 나타내는 서술격 조사.

A predicate particle indicating the meaning of the attribute or category

of the thing that the subject of the sentence refers to.

서울로 가는 비행기를 놓칠 뻔했어!

I almost missed my flight to Seoul.

"다행이야"

네가 고소당하지 않아서 정말 마음이 놓여.

I'm so relieved that you weren't sued.

"다행이야"

의사 말이 걔는 곧 괜찮아질 거래요.

The doctor say she'll be back to normal
in no time.

"다행이에요"

그 프로젝트는 결국 잘 해결되었어.

The project worked out well in the end.

"다행이야"

알람이 안 울려서 늦잠을 잤어요.
하지만 회사에 늦진 않았어요.

I overslept because my alarm didn't go off.

But I made it to work on time.

"다행이에요"

방금 고속도로에서 사고가 날 뻔했는데,
길이 너무 미끄러워서 그런가?

I almost got an accident in highway just

before, is it because the road is so slippery?

"다행이야"

반갑다

[반갑따] [bangaptta]

* 보고 싶던 사람을 만나거나 원하는 일이 이루어져서 마음이 즐겁고 기쁘다.

Joyful and happy as one meets a person that one missed.

●

반가워

[반가워] [bangawo]

반가워요

[반가워요] [bangawoyo]

●

드디어 여름 방학이 끝나고 우리 반 친구들과
선생님들을 다시 만났어요.
Summer vacation is finally over and I
met my classmates and teachers again.

"반가워요"

온라인에서 만난 한국 친구가 있어.
네가 지혜구나!
드디어 이렇게 직접 만나게 돼서 너무 좋다!
I have a Korean friend I met online.
You must be Jihye! It's nice to finally
meet you in person!

"반가워"

오랜만에 친구를 만났어. 이게 얼마 만이야!
I met a friend after a long time.
It's been so long!

"반가워"

우린 부산 호텔의 로비에서 우연히 만났어.
이게 누구야!
We met by chance in the lobby of Busan
hotel. Look who's here!

"반가워"

평소 이름만 전해 듣다가 직접 만나니 좋네요.
It's nice to put a face to the name.

"반가워요"

기쁘다

[기쁘다] [gippeuda]

* 기분이 매우 좋고 즐겁다.
Feeling very good and in a good mood.

기뻐

[기뻐] [gippeo]

기뻐요

[기뻐요] [gippeoyo]

거의 3년이 걸리긴 했는데
끝끝내 공인회계사 시험에 합격했어.
It took me almost 3 years
but at long last I passed my CPA exam.

"기뻐"

점점 더 많은 외국인들이 한국어를 배우고
있다고 들었어요.
I heard that more and more foreigners
are learning the Korean language.

"(한국인 입장에서) 기뻐요"

우리 여동생은 마침내 자기 방을 갖게 되었어.
My younger sister finally has her own room.

"기뻐"

너 많은 사람들 앞에서 말하는 걸 두려워하더니
이제 극복했구나.
I can tell that you've overcome your fear
of public speaking.

"기뻐"

네가 다시 즐거워하는 것을 보니 정말 좋아.
It sure is nice to see you having fun again

"기뻐"

엄마! 저 취직해서 다음 주 월요일부터 출근해요!
Mom! I got the job and I start work next
Monday!

"기뻐요"

좋다

[조ː타] [joːta]

* 감정 등이 기쁘고 흐뭇하다.

Having a feeling, etc., of happiness and satisfaction.

●

좋아

[조ː아] [joːa]

좋아요

[조ː아요] [joːayo]

●

난 하루 종일 K-pop을 듣고 있어!

I've been listening to K-pop all day.

"좋아"

날씨가 너무 좋아서 집까지 걸어갔어.

It was a lovely day so I walked home.

"좋아"

시원한 맥주 한 잔에 하루의 피로가 말끔히 풀렸어.

A glass of cold beer relieved my fatigue from the day's work.

"좋아"

오랜만에 친구들을 만나 수다를 떨었어.

I met my friends and chatted with them for the first time in a long time.

"좋아"

날씨가 진짜 좋아서 노천카페에서 점심을 먹고 있어.

The weather is so nice, so I'm having lunch at the sidewalk cafe.

"좋아"

걔 생각만 해도 가슴이 두근거려.

Just the thought of her made my heart flutter.

"좋아"

재미있다

[재미읻따] [jaemiittta]

* 즐겁고 유쾌한 느낌이 있다.

Feelings of joy and pleasantness being present.

●

재미있어

[재미이써] [jaemiisseo]

재미있어요

[재미이써요] [jaemiisseoyo]

●

◎ 재미있다 vs 즐겁다

· 재미있다 : 아기자기한 즐거운 느낌이 있는 마음.
  주로 말할 때 '~은/는/이/가 재미있다'라고 합니다. 모든 물건, 상황, 행동에
  사용할 수 있습니다.
  Sensing pleasure from small matters. This is usually spoken as
  '~is interesting.' It can be used for all things, situations, and actions.

· 즐겁다 : 신경 쓰이는 것 없이 행복하고 기쁘다.
  Happy and pleased without having anything that bothers you.

이 책은 수년 전에 출판되었지만 30번을 넘게 읽어도 여전히 작가의 이야기와 코믹한 포인트가 대단한 것 같아요.
I know it was published many years ago but even after its 30th reading, her story-telling and comic timing is still great.

"재미있어요"

여가 시간에 친구들과 함께 X-Box 하는 것을 좋아해.
When I do have free time, I like to play X-Box with my friends.

"재미있어"

걔의 웃긴 행동을 보고 모두가 웃었어.
His comical movements had everyone laughing.

"재미있어"

할머니께선 종종 재미난 옛날이야기를 들려주시곤 하셨어요.
My grandmother often used to tell us great old time stories.

"재미있어요"

우린 넷플릭스를 보느라 시간 가는 줄 몰랐어.
We lost track of time watching Netflix.

"재미있어"

즐겁다

[즐겁따] [jeulgeoptta]

* 마음에 들어 흐뭇하고 기쁘다.
Pleased and satisfied with something.

●

즐거워

[즐거워] [jeulgeowo]

즐거워요

[즐거워요] [jeulgeowoyo]

●

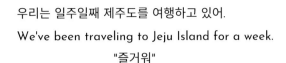

우리는 일주일째 제주도를 여행하고 있어.
We've been traveling to Jeju Island for a week.
"즐거워"

지금 친구들과 만나서 먹고 마시고
즐거운 시간을 보내고 있는 중이야.
Right now, I've met my friends and we're
having a pleasant time eating and drinking.
"즐거워"

남동생과 함께 어린 시절 사진첩을 보다가
옛 추억이 떠올라서 깔깔 웃었어.
While looking at my childhood photo album
with my younger brother, I laughed out loud
at the thought of old memories.
"즐거워"

한국의 가장 큰 명절 중 하나인 추석에는
온 가족이 모여 맛있는 음식을 먹고 대화를 나눠요.
During Chuseok, one of the biggest holidays in
Korea, the whole family gathers to eat delicious
food and talk to each other.
"즐거워요"

요즘 바빠서 가족들과 보낼 시간이 없었는데,
오늘은 가족들과 한강공원에 가서 자전거도 타고
치킨도 시켜 먹으면서 즐거운 시간을 보내고 있어요.
I've been busy lately, so I didn't have time to
spend with my family. But today, I'm having a
good time with my family at Hangang Park,
riding a bicycle and also eating delivered chicken.
"즐거워요"

홀가분하다

[홀가분하다] [holgabunhada]

* 신경이 쓰이거나 귀찮지 않고 가볍고 편안하다.

Feeling light and comfortable without being burdened
or bothered by something.

●

홀가분해

[홀가분해] [holgabunhae]

홀가분해요

[홀가분해요] [holgabunhaeyo]

●

마감 시간 직전에 보고서를 제출했어요.

I turned in my report just under the wire.

"홀가분해요"

우린 가방이 많아서 기차역에 있는 짐 보관함에
가방들을 넣었어요.

We had a lot of bags, so we put them
in the luggage locker at the train station.

"홀가분해"

이번 주에 할 일이 산더미 같았지만, 드디어
오늘 다 끝내고 가벼운 마음으로 집에 가고 있어!

I've had a lot of work to do this week, but
I've finally got it all done today and am
going home with a light heart!

"홀가분해"

걘 처음엔 부인했지만 마침내 사실을 털어놓았어.

She denied it at first but finally come clean.

"홀가분해"

난 어렸을 때부터 가난해서 항상 부자가 되어야 한
다고 생각했어. 그래서 항상 돈에 대해 집착해왔어.
하지만 이제 돈에 대한 욕심을 버렸어.

I've been poor since I was young, so I always
thought I should be rich.

So I've been obsessed with money at all times.

But now I'm not greedy about money.

"홀가분해"

상쾌하다

[상ː쾌하다] [sang:kwaehada]

* 기분이나 느낌 등이 시원하고 산뜻하다.
Feeling cool and fresh.

●

상쾌해

[상ː쾌해] [sang:kwaehae]

상쾌해요

[상ː쾌해요] [sang:kwaehaeyo]

●

우린 바다에 도착해서 해변으로 내달렸어요.
We arrived at the sea and ran to the beach.
"상쾌해요"

우린 깨끗하고 신선한 공기를 마시며
수목원을 산책하고 있어.
We're strolling in the arboretum breathing
clean and fresh air.
"상쾌해"

약간 더워서 땀이 살짝 났는데 시원하고 부드러운
바람이 불어와서 땀을 식혀주었어. 부드럽게 불어
오는 바람을 쐬면서 공원에 앉아 있을 때 드는 마음.
It was a little hot, so I sweated a little, but a
cool, soft breeze blew and cooled my sweat.
The feeling you get when you sit in the park
while enjoying the gentle breeze.
"상쾌해"

그동안 미뤄왔던 대청소를 했어요. 대청소를
다 하고 나서 깨끗해진 집을 볼 때 드는 마음.
I did a spring cleaning that I've been putting
off. This is how I feel when I see the house
cleaned after all the spring cleaning.
"상쾌해요"

오늘 열대야라서 잘 수가 없어.
더운 여름날 기분 전환을 위해 차가운 물로 샤워하고
나왔을 때 드는 마음.
I can't sleep due to a heatwave going on today.
This is how I feel when I take a cold shower
for a mood change on a hot summer day.
"상쾌해"

유쾌하다

[유쾌하다] [yukwaehada]

* 기분이나 느낌 등이 시원하고 산뜻하다.

Feeling cool and fresh.

●

유쾌해

[유쾌해] [yukwaehae]

유쾌해요

[유쾌해요] [yukwaehaeyo]

●

선생님께선 웃으시며 아이들과 재미있는
이야기를 나누고 계셨어요.
The teacher was laughing and joking
with the children.

"유쾌해요"

그들은 정말 좋은 가족이에요.
그는 항상 밝게 웃으며 안부 인사를 해요.
They are a very nice family, he always
smiles brightly and says hello.

"유쾌해요"

친구들과 같이 재미있는 영화를 볼 때면 너무
웃겨서 배가 아파 죽을 것 같아.
When I watch a fun movie with my friends,
it's so funny that my stomach hurts.

"유쾌해"

친구들과 수다를 떨고 나니 스트레스가 풀렸어.
기분이 좋아진 난 웃으며 휘파람까지 불었어.
After chatting with my friends, my stress
was relieved. Feeling better, I smiled and
even whistled.

"유쾌해"

걘 언제나 긍정적이고 낙천적이야. 그래서 걔랑
함께 있으면 너무 즐거워서 웃음을 멈출 수 없어.
He's always so positive and optimistic.
So when I'm with him, I can't stop laughing
because that time is so enjoyable.

"유쾌해"

통쾌하다

[통ː쾌하다] [tongkwaehada]

* 아주 즐겁고 속이 시원하다.

Very pleasant and feeling good.

●

통쾌해

[통ː쾌해] [tongkwaehae]

통쾌해요

[통쾌ː해요] [tongkwaehaeyo]

●

그 선수는 9회 말에 홈런을 쳤어요.

The player hit a home run in the
bottom of the ninth inning.

"통쾌해요"

그 팀은 마침내 모든 어려움을 이겨내고
우승을 차지했어요!

The team finally overcame all difficulties
and won the title!

"통쾌해요"

걘 소신 있게 상사가 그동안 잘못해오고
있던 일들을 따끔하게 충고했어.

She admonished with conviction what
her boss had been doing wrong.

"통쾌해"

이 영화에서 피해자는 마침내 범인에게 복수해.

The victim finally had her revenge on the
criminal in this movie.

"통쾌해"

걘 항상 내 발차기 실력을 무시했어.
하지만 난 개랑 겨루기를 해서 태권도 대회에서
우승했어.

He always ignored my kick skills.
But I competed with him and won the
Taekwondo competition.

"통쾌해"

쌤통

[쌤ː통] [ssaemːtong]

쌤통 + 이다 = 쌤통이다 [쌤ː통이다] [ssaemːtongida]

평소에 미워하던 사람이 잘못되는 것을 보고 속이 시원하고 기분이 좋다.

Feeling satisfied to hear that a person you have been
hating has fallen into a bad situation.

Being happy to hear about someone's misfortune.

●

쌤통이다

[쌤ː통이다] [ssaemːtongida]

쌤통이에요

[쌤ː통이에요] [ssaemːtongieyo]

●

◎ -이다 [이다] [ida]

주어가 지시하는 대상의 속성이나 부류를 지정하는 뜻을 나타내는 서술격 조사.

A predicate particle indicating the meaning of the attribute or category

of the thing that the subject of the sentence refers to.

걔는 계속 자기 실력을 자랑하더니 예선전도
통과하지 못했어.

She had kept bragging about her skill
but terrifically failed to get through the
preliminaries.

"쌤통이다"

걔는 오만하게 굴더니 시험에서 떨어졌어.

She acted so arrogantly but she failed
the test.

"쌤통이다"

걘 맨날 잘난 척하더니 오늘 시험에서
커닝하다가 걸렸어.

He's such a know-it-all. But today he got
caught cheating on the test.

"쌤통이다"

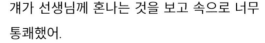

걔는 나한테 항상 못되게 굴어.

걔 이번에 관리직으로 승진 못 했대.

He's always mean to me. I heard he didn't
get promoted to a management position
this time.

"쌤통이다"

걔가 선생님께 혼나는 것을 보고 속으로 너무
통쾌했어.

I took great inward pleasure in seeing that
rascal get into trouble with the teacher.

"쌤통이다"

분노

ANGER

야속하다

[야ː소카다] [yaːsokada]

어떤 사람이나 어떤 것이 정(情)이 없이 행동을 하는 것에 대해
섭섭하여 기분이 좋지 않다.
Someone or something's quality of being cold and
heartless due to the lack of love for others,
thereby making one feel unhappy and displeased.

●

야속해

[야ː소캐] [yaːsokae]

야속해요

[야ː소캐요] [yaːsokaeyo]

●

내 여자친구는 내 진심을 몰라줬어.
My girlfriend failed to understand
my true intention.

"야속해"

나이가 들수록 시간이 정말 빨리 가요.
As I get older, Time flies so fast.

"(세월이) 야속해요"

걔는 내 부탁을 단칼에 거절했어.
He flatly refused my request.

"야속해"

내 친구는 내가 카페로 돌아왔을 때
냉정하게 대했어.
My friend gave me a frosty welcome
when I returned to the cafe.

"야속해"

그 DJ는 내 신청곡을 냉정하게 거절했어요.
The DJ emotionlessly rejected my song
request.

"야속해요"

너랑 같이 한잔하고 싶지만, 이 제안서들을
마무리해야 해.
I'd like to join you for a drink, but I've
got to get these proposals finished.

"(일이 많아서) 야속해"

억울하다

[어굴하다] [eogulhada]

* 잘못한 것도 없이 피해를 입어 속이 상하고 답답하다.

Feeling distressed and frustrated because one has suffered damage although one did not do anything wrong.

●

억울해

[어굴해] [eogulhae]

억울해요

[어굴해요] [eogulhaeyo]

●

진짜 이거 내가 한 것 아니야.
정말이라니까, 난 누명을 쓴 거야.
I really didn't do this.
Believe me when I tell you,
I've been framed.

　　　　　"억울해"

가: 너 상사한테 내 욕하고 다닌다며?
나: 아냐, 안 했어. 아무도 안 믿어주네.
A: I heard you were badmouthing me
　　to the boss.
B: No, I didn't. No one believes me.

　　　　　"억울해"

내 남동생이 말썽을 부렸는데 왜 나도
혼나는 건지 모르겠어. 난 아무 짓도 안 했어!
My younger brother was acting up,
but I don't know why I also got scolded
by mom. I had nothing to do with it!

　　　　　"억울해"

우리 고양이가 우리 엄마의 값비싼 골동품 화분
을 깼어요. 하지만 집으로 돌아오신 우리 엄마는
의심스러운 눈초리로 저를 쳐다보셨어요.
My cat broke my mom's expensive antique
vase. But when my mom came home, she
looked at me with suspicious eyes.

　　　　　"억울해요"

원망스럽다

[원ː망스럽따] [wonːmangseureoptta]

* 마음에 들지 않아서 탓하거나 미워하는 마음이 있다.

Having the mind of blaming or hating something or someone because one is displeased with it or him/her.

●

원망스러워

[원ː망스러워] [wonːmangseureowo]

원망스러워요

[원ː망스러워요] [wonːmangseureowoyo]

●

◎ -스럽다 [쓰럽따] [seureoptta]

명사 뒤에 붙어 '그러한 성질이 있음'의 뜻을 더하고, 형용사로 만드는 단어.

This word is attached after a noun and adds the meaning of 'having such attributes' so that the noun becomes an adjective.

넌 내 마음을 엉망으로 만들어놓고 있어.

You are messing with my mind.

"원망스러워"

힘든 일은 다 내가 했어. 그런데 네가 모든
공을 다 차지했어.

I did all the hard work. But you took
all the credit.

"원망스러워"

우리 엄마는 암으로 투병 중이셔.
그런데 오늘 우리 아빠가 교통사고를 당하셨어.
왜 나한테만 이런 일이 자꾸 생기는 거야?

My mom is battling cancer.

But today, my dad had a car accident.

Why do these things keep happening to me?

"(하늘이) 원망스러워"

폭우와 홍수로 벼 수확을 망쳤는데 한 달째
비가 계속 내리고 있어요.

Heavy rains and floods ruined the rice harvest.

But it's been raining for a month.

"(하늘이) 원망스러워요"

넌 아직도 팀 프로젝트가 실패한 게 내 잘못이라고
생각하는구나. 우리 다 같이 한 거잖아.
나 혼자 한 게 아니라고!

You still think it's my fault to fail in the group
project. We all did it together.

I didn't do it alone!

"원망스러워"

힘들다

[힘들다] [himdeulda]

* 마음이 쓰이거나 수고가 되는 면이 있다.
Requiring much attention and effort.

힘들어

[힘드러] [himdeureo]

힘들어요

[힘드러요] [himdeureoyo]

새로운 언어를 배우는 것은 쉽지 않아요.

It's not easy learning a new language.

"힘들어요"

요즘 많은 일을 겪고 있어. 사는 게 고달프네.

I'm going through a lot right now.

Life is tough.

"힘들어"

회사에서 너무 스트레스를 받았어요. 상사는 엄청나게 일을 시키고 항상 날 힘들게 해요.

I was under so much pressure at work.

My boss is such a slave driver and always gives me a hard time.

"힘들어요"

아이를 키우면서 하루 종일 일하는 것은 쉽지 않아. 우리 남편은 도와주지도 않아.

It's not easy to work all day raising a kid.

My husband doesn't even help me.

"힘들어"

우리 할아버지께서 돌아가셨다는 소식을 들었을 때 얼마나 울었는지 몰라.

You have no idea how much I cried when I heard that my grandfather passed away.

"힘들어"

거북하다

[거ː부카다] [geoːbukada]

* 1. 움직임이나 몸의 기능이 자연스럽지 못하거나 불편한 느낌이 있다.

Feeling unnatural or uncomfortable in moving

or carrying out bodily functions.

* 2. 마음이 불편하거나 어색하다.

Feeling uncomfortable or strained.

●

거북해

[거ː부캐] [geoːbukae]

거북해요

[거ː부캐요] [geoːbukaeyo]

●

어떤 남자가 나를 뚫어지게 쳐다봤어요.

Some guy looked at me with piercing eyes.

"거북해요"

이번 주에 술을 너무 많이 마셨어.

그래서 술 생각만 해도 속이 안 좋아.

I've been drinking too much this week.

So I feel sick just thinking about drinking.

"거북해"

걔는 내 앞에서 내가 싫어하는 사람들 이야기를

계속해. 난 정말 걔네들 이야기 듣고 싶지 않아.

He keeps talking about people I don't like

in front of me.

I really don't want to hear about them.

"거북해"

배가 고파서 밥을 급하게 먹었더니 속이 불편해요.

I ate in a hurry because I was hungry,

so my stomach feels uncomfortable.

"거북해요"

지난 주말에 내 친구와 크게 다퉜어.

걔랑 화해도 안 했고 아직 엄청 화가 나 있는데,

오늘 쇼핑몰에서 우연히 걔를 마주쳤어.

My friend and I had a big fight last weekend.

I didn't make up with her and I was still very

angry, but I ran into her at the mall today.

"거북해"

괴롭다

[괴롭따/궤롭따] [goeroptta/gweroptta]

* 몸이나 마음이 편하지 않고 아프고 고통스럽다.
Feeling pain in one's body or mind. suffering

●

괴로워

[괴로워/궤로워] [goerowo/gwerowo]

괴로워요

[괴로워요/궤로워요] [goerowoyo/gwerowoyo]

●

난 오늘 면접을 완전히 망쳐버렸어.

I so blew the job interview today.

"괴로워"

나는 사업이 망해서 빚더미에 올라앉았어.

I am in serious debt because my business collapsed.

"괴로워"

배가 너무 아파서 한숨도 못 잤어.

I was up all night with pretty extreme stomach pain.

"괴로워"

코로나로 인한 폐쇄 명령 때문에 우리 가게는 망했어요.

My store was ruined because of the shut-down order that was issued due to COVID-19.

"괴로워요"

우리 부모님께선 이혼하셨고 우리 엄마와 언니는 매일 싸워요.

My parents are divorced and my mother and older sister are always fighting.

"괴로워요"

난 은행에 빚이 많아.

안타깝게도, 오늘 직장에서 해고당했어.

My bank account is deep in the red.

Unfortunately, I was fired from my job today.

"괴로워"

부럽다

[부럽따] [bureoptta]

* 다른 사람의 일이나 물건이 좋아 보여 자기도 그런 일을 이루거나
물건을 갖기를 바라는 마음이 있다.

Desiring to achieve or possess the same kind of feat or thing
that others have achieved or possess because they look good.

●

부러워

[부러워][bureowo]

부러워요

[부러워요][bureowoyo]

●

개는 젊음과 활기가 넘쳐.

He is full of youth and vitality.

"부러워"

넌 잘생기고 공부도 잘하고 운동도 잘해.

You're good looking, very good at
studying, and even good at sports.

"부러워"

그의 가족은 언제나 화목하고 행복해요.

His family is always harmony and happy.

"부러워"

우리 형은 이제 막 고등학교를 졸업하고
대학생이 되었어요.

My older brother just graduated from a
high school and became a college student.

"부러워요"

우리 부모님께서는 한국으로 휴가를 가셨어요.

My parents went on vacation to Korea.

"부러워요"

나는 외동이야. 내 친구 민수는 두 명의 자매와
한 명의 형제가 있어.

I'm an only child. My friend Minsu has two
sisters and a brother.

"부러워"

질투하다

[질투하다] [jiltuhada]

* 1. 부부나 애인 사이에서 상대방이 다른 사람을 좋아할 경우에
지나치게 미워하고 싫어하다.
To hate and dislike toward one's spouse or lover
when he/she likes someone else.
* 2. 다른 사람이 잘되거나 좋은 처지에 있는 것을 괜히 미워하고 싫어하다.
To hate or dislike a person better than oneself.

●

질투나

[질투나] [jiltuna]

질투 나요

[질투나요] [jiltunayo]

●

걘 아버지 덕분에 승승장구했어.

She has had success after success
thanks to her father.

"질투나"

그는 회사 내 인맥을 통해 고속 승진했어요.

He was given a speedy promotion
because of a personal connection with
someone higher up.

"질투 나요"

걔는 예쁘고 성격도 좋아.

She is very pretty and has a nice personality.

"질투나"

난 내 여자친구가 남사친¹을 만나는 것을 좋아
하지 않아요. 내 여자친구는 내일 걔들과 커피를
마시러 갈 거래요.

I don't like my girlfriend meeting her male
friends. She's going to drink coffee with
them tomorrow.

"질투 나요"

우리 엄마는 오빠를 칭찬하기 시작하셨어.
사실 나도 같이 했는데.

My mom started praising my older brother.
Actually did it with him too.

"질투 나요"

---

1. 남사친 : 남자 사람 친구의 줄임말. An abbreviation of 'a male friend'

거슬리다

[거슬리다] [geoseullida]

* 못마땅하거나 마음에 들지 않아 기분이 상하다.

To feel bad due to displeasure or dissatisfaction with something.

●

거슬려

[거슬려] [geoseullyeo]

거슬려요

[거슬려요] [geoseullyeoyo]

●

지하철 안에서 학생들이 시끄럽게
떠드는 소리가 들려요.
I can hear students talking loudly
in the subway.

"거슬려요"

도서관에 갔는데 내 옆에 있는 어떤 남자가
미친 듯이 다리를 떨어. 너무 산만해.
When I went to the library, a man next to me
shook his legs like crazy. It's so distracting.

"거슬려"

걔는 라면을 후루룩거리면서 먹고 있었어.
걔는 먹을 때 너무 소리를 많이 내!
He was slurping his ramen.
He makes way too much noise while eating!

"거슬려"

밥을 먹다가 흰 원피스에 김치를 흘렸어요.
I spilled kimchi on a white dress while eating.

"거슬려요"

걔는 항상 말투가 퉁명스러워서 화난 것 같아.
걔랑 대화할 때마다 기분이 안 좋아.
She appears to be mad because she always
talks bluntly.
I don't feel good whenever I'm talking to her.

"거슬려"

귀찮다

[귀찬타] [gwichanta]

* 싫고 성가시다.

Disliking and feeling tired of doing something.

●

귀찮아

[귀차나] [gwichana]

귀찮아요

[귀차나요] [gwichanayo]

●

난 아무것도 하고 싶지 않아.

I don't feel like doing anything.

"귀찮아"

아이들이 새 게임을 사 달라고 계속 졸라요.

The kids keep pestering me to buy them
a new game.

"귀찮아"

잔디를 깎아야 하는데 오늘은 귀찮아서 못 깎겠어.

The grass needs cutting.

But I can't be bothered to do it today.

"귀찮아"

사람들이 계속 똑같은 질문을 해요.

People keep asking me the same questions
over and over.

"귀찮아요"

그 옷은 다림질해야 하는데 피곤해서
아무것도 하기가 싫어요.

That needs to be ironed.

But I'm tired, not want to do anything.

"귀찮아요"

손빨래 진짜 싫어. 정말 번거로워.

I hate hand washing clothes. Such a hassle.

"귀찮아"

짜증

[짜증] [jjajeung]

짜증 + 나다 = 짜증 나다 [짜증나다] [jjajeungnada]

* 마음에 들지 않아서 화를 내거나 싫은 느낌을 겉으로 드러내는 일.
또는 그런 성미.

An act of expressing one's anger or dislike towards something
because one is dissatisfied, or such a disposition.

●

짜증 나

[짜증나] [jjajeungna]

짜증 나요

[짜증나요] [jjajeungnayo]

●

◎ -나다 [나다] [nada]

* 어떤 감정이나 느낌이 생기다.

To feel a certain emotion or sensation.

개는 내가 하는 일에 사사건건 간섭해.

She meddled in everything I did.

"짜증 나"

에어컨이 또 고장 났어! 어제 고친 건데!

The air conditioner is broken again!

I just had it fixed yesterday!

"짜증 나"

개는 바쁘다는 둥 아프다는 둥
핑계를 대면서 약속을 지키지 않아.

He never keeps his promises, saying he is
too busy or he is not well or something.

"짜증 나"

자고 있는데 모기가 귀 옆에서 계속 왱왱거렸어.

I was sleeping and the mosquito kept
buzzing in my ears.

"짜증 나"

난 우리 여동생과 코드가 맞지 않고,
우린 모든 일에 부딪쳐요.

I don't get along with my younger sister,
and we argue about everything.

"짜증 나요"

걘 자기가 얼마나 돈이 많은지 자랑했어.

She boasted about how much money she had.

"짜증 나"

불쾌하다

[불쾌하다] [bulkwaehada]

* 어떤 일이 마음에 들지 않아 기분이 좋지 않다.

Feeling bad due to dissatisfaction with a certain matter.

불쾌해

[불쾌해] [bulkwaehae]

불쾌해요

[불쾌해요] [bulkwaehaeyo]

넌 우리 엄마가 아니야. 너 선 넘은 것 같아.

You're not my mother.

I think you've crossed the line here.

"불쾌해"

넌 내 친절함을 이용하고 있어.

You're taking advantage of my kindness.

"불쾌해"

그 사람 좀 공격적이라 처음 만났을 때 사람들이
비호감이라고 느껴.

He's slightly aggressive, which a lot of people
find off-putting when they first meet him.

"불쾌해"

우린 어제 싸웠고 오늘 내가 문자했는데,
보다시피 읽씹¹했네.

We had a fight yesterday and I texted her
this morning but obviously, she left me on read.

"불쾌해"

정말 습하고 더운 날씨예요.

It's really humid and hot.

"불쾌해요"

걔 반응은 애매모호하고 무시하는 듯했어요.

Her response was non-committal and dismissive.

"불쾌해요"

---

1. 읽씹 : '읽고 씹다'의 준말. 문자나 메신저, 소셜미디어의 메시지 내용을 읽었음에도 아무런 답신을 하지 않는 경우를 이르는 속어.

An abbreviation of 'read and chew.' A slang that refers to a case where you read messages on texts, messengers, or social media but do not reply.

화나다

[화ː나다] [hwaːnada]

* 몹시 언짢거나 못마땅하여 기분이 나빠지다.

To feel bad, being extremely upset or unhappy.

●

화나

[화:나] [hwaːna]

화나요

[화:나요] [hwaːnayo]

●

난 네 건방진 태도가 이제 지긋지긋해.

I've had enough of your cocky attitude.

"화나"

지호는 자신이 불합리하게 굴고 있다는
말에 분했어.

Jiho took umbrage at the suggestion
that he was being unreasonable.

"화나"

걔는 약속에 늦었어. 하지만 사과도 안 했어.

She's late for an appointment.
But she didn't even apologize.

"화나"

걔는 내가 하는 말마다 빈정거려요.

He talks sarcastically to everything I say.

"화나요"

넌 공격적일 정도로 무례했어.

You were rude to the point of being
aggressive.

"화나"

한강에서 자전거를 타려고 했는데
걔는 나를 바람 맞혔어.

We planned to ride a bicycle at the
Han river, but she stood me up.

"화나"

열받다

[열받따] [yeolbattta]

열 + 받다 = 열받다

사람이 감정의 자극을 받거나 격분하다.

A person is stimulated by emotions and is furious.

열받아

[열바다] [yeolbada]

열받아요

[열바다요] [yeolbadayo]

◎ 열 [열] [yeol]

* 매우 화가 나거나 흥분한 상태.

The state of being furious or agitated.

◎ -받다 [받따] [battta]

* 어떤 상황이 자기에게 미치다.

To be affected by a situation

넌 내 결혼식을 다 망쳤어.

나 충분히 참을 만큼 참았어.

You ruined my wedding.

I've had it up to here with you.

"열받아"

직장을 잃은 것도 모자라서 쫓겨나기까지

한 건 도를 넘었어.

Losing my job was bad enough,

but being evicted was the final straw.

"열받아"

그 사람이 내 아이 앞에서 나한테 욕설을

퍼붓기 시작했어.

He started hurling abuse at me

in front of my child.

"열받아"

네가 나한테 한 짓 중에 가장 굴욕적인 짓이야!

This is the most humiliating thing

you've ever done to me!

"열받아"

또 상사랑 싸웠다니까. 정말 짜증 나!

도대체 왜 그 사람은 그렇게 내 험담을

해 대는지 알 수가 없어.

I had an argument with my boss again.

What a bummer! I don't understand

why he's bad-mouthing me.

"열받아"

역겹다

[역겹따] [yeokkkyeoptta]

* 1. 맛이나 냄새 등이 매우 나쁘고 싫어 토할 것처럼 메스껍다.
Feeling nausea because the taste, smell, etc., of something is very
bad and sickening.
* 2. 몹시 언짢거나 마음에 들지 않아 기분이 나쁘다.
Feeling bad and unpleased because one does not like something.

●

역겨워

[역껴워] [yeokkkyeowo]

역겨워요

[역껴워요] [yeokkkyeowoyo]

●

으윽 ~ 이거 무슨 냄새야?

마트에서 생선을 사 왔는데 그게 상했나 봐.

온 집안이 썩은 생선 냄새로 가득 찼어.

Eww~ What's this smell?

I bought some fish from the mart,

but it must have gone bad.

The whole house stinks with rotten fish odor.

"역겨워"

걔는 사람들 앞에서는 온갖 착한 척을 다 하지만

뒤에서는 호박씨를 까요.

She pretends to be all nice in front of people,

but she's entirely different behind their back.

"역겨워요"

내 여자친구가 내 가장 친한 친구와 바람났어.

"넌 내 가장 친한 친구야!

어떻게 나한테 이럴 수 있어?"

My girlfriend cheated on me with my best

friend.

"You are my best friend!

How could you do this to me?"

"역겨워"

그 살인자는 자신이 한 짓에 대해 후회하는

기색을 전혀 보이지 않았어. 반성하기는커녕

법정에서 웃고 있었어.

The murderer gave no sign of regret about

what he had done. He was smiling at the

court, let alone reflecting on himself.

"역겨워"

얄밉다

[얄밉따] [yalmiptta]

* 다른 사람이 하는 행동이나 말 등이 싫거나 밉다.

Someone's behavior, way of speaking, etc., being unpleasant or detestable.

●

얄미워

[얄미워] [yalmiwo]

얄미워요

[얄미워요] [yalmiwoyo]

●

엄마한테 혼나고 있는데 여동생이
날 보고 웃고 있어.
My mom is scolding me,
but my younger sister is smiling at me.
"얄미워"

걘 말할 때마다 자기자랑만 늘어놔요.
She always brags about herself
whenever she speaks.
"얄미워요"

내 여동생은 내가 학교에서 잘못한 일들만
엄마한테 고자질해요.
My younger sister tells my mom about
what I did wrong at school.
"얄미워요"

걔 말투는 짜증 나.
내가 시험에서 떨어지기를 바라는 것 같아.
Her way of speaking is annoying. It seemed
like she wanted me to fail the exam.
"얄미워"

걔는 자신에게 유리한 방향으로 이야기했어.
He spoke in a way that was favorable to him.
"얄미워"

걔는 항상 술값 내기 전에 어떻게든 몰래 빠져나가.
He always manages to sneak out before paying
for the drink.
"얄미워"

밉다

[밉따] [miptta]

* 행동이나 태도 등이 마음에 들지 않거나 기분이 나쁜 느낌이 있다.
(for behavior, attitude, etc.) Annoying or irritating.

●

미워

[미워] [miwo]

미워요

[미워요] [miwoyo]

●

갠 자기가 잘못해놓고 계속 변명만
늘어놓고 있어.
He's the one who made a mistake,
but all he does is make excuses.

"미워"

어제 걔랑 말다툼했어. 걘 오늘 학교에서
하루 종일 날 투명 인간 취급하더라.
I had an argument with him yesterday.
He treated me like an invisible man
all day at school today.

"미워"

내가 모든 사실을 뻔히 알고 있는데 넌 상황을
모면하려고 계속 거짓말만 하는구나!
I know all the facts, but you keep lying
to escape the situation!

"미워"

다이어트 중인데 넌 내 앞에서 계속 라면이랑
치킨을 먹고 있어.
I'm dieting, but you keep eating ramen
and chicken in front of me.

"미워"

우리 할아버지께선 갑자기 화를 버럭 내시며
절 혼내셨어요. 전 아무것도 안 했어요!
My grandpa suddenly lost his temper
and scolded me. I didn't do anything!

"미워요"

심술

[심술] [simsul]

심술 + 나다 = 심술 나다 [심술 나다] [simsulnada]

* 그럴 만한 이유 없이 못되게 굴거나 고집을 부리는 마음.

The attitude of behaving badly or being obstinate without reason.

심술 나

[심술나] [simsulna]

심술 나요

[심술나요] [simsulnayo]

◎ -나다 [나다] [nada]

* 어떤 감정이나 느낌이 생기다.

To feel a certain emotion or sensation.

우리 아들이 축구 경기에서 졌어.
그리곤 괜히 축구공을 화단으로 뻥 차버렸어.
My son lost the soccer game.
Then he kicked the soccer ball into
the flower bed for no reason.
                "심술 나"

상사한테 동료가 계속 칭찬을 받아요.
난 이유 없이 동료에게 짜증을 냈어요.
My boss always compliments my colleague.
I acted irritated toward him for no reason.
                "심술 나요"

남자친구와 말다툼했어. 난 집에 와서 엄마한테
아무것도 먹지 않겠다고 괜히 고집을 부렸어.
I bickered with my boyfriend.
When I got home, I got stubborn and
protested to my mom that I wouldn't eat
anything.
                "심술 나"

우리 엄마는 맨날 나만 보면 공부하라는 말만 해.
그래서 일부러 이번 시험을 망친 거야.
My mom always tells me to study whenever
she sees me. That's why I messed up this
test on purpose.
                "심술 나"

실망하다

[실망하다] [silmanghada]

* 기대하던 대로 되지 않아 희망을 잃거나 마음이 몹시 상하다.

To lose hope or feel hurt because something did not work out.

실망했어

[실망해써] [silmanghaesseo]

실망했어요

[실망해써요] [silmanghaesseoyo]

넌 절대 네 잘못을 인정하지 않는구나.
부끄러운 줄 알아!
You never admit your mistake.
Shame on you!
"실망했어"

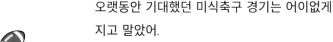

오랫동안 기대했던 미식축구 경기는 어이없게
지고 말았어.
The football game that I had been
looking forward to for a long time ended
up a ridiculous loss.
"실망했어"

널 정말 믿었는데 넌 나한테 모든 걸 속였어.
I really believed in you, but you lied to me
about everything.
"실망했어"

이럴 줄 알면서도 왜 말 안 했어?
네가 모든 공을 차지하려고? 너 진짜 비겁하다!
Why didn't you tell me even though you
knew this would happen? You wanted to
take all the credit? You're such a coward!
"실망했어"

이번 달에 회사에서 우리 팀 모두에게 보너스를
준다는 소문이 있었는데 모두 사실이 아니었어요.
There were rumors that the company would
give bonuses to all of our team this month,
but none of them were true.
"실망했어요"

놀라움

SURPRISE

놀라다

[놀ː라다] [nolːrada]

* 기대하던 대로 되지 않아 희망을 잃거나 마음이 몹시 상하다.

To lose hope or feel hurt because something did not work out.

●

놀랐어

[놀ː라써] [nolːrasseo]

놀랐어요

[놀ː라써요] [nolːrasseoyo]

●

◎ 이 표현은 부사 '깜짝'과 사용되는 경우가 많다.

This expression is often used with the adverb '깜짝 (all of a sudden).'

◎ 깜짝 [깜짝] [kkamjjak]

* 갑자기 놀라는 모양.

In the manner of being surprised suddenly.

운전을 하고 있었는데 갑자기 고양이가
도로로 뛰어들었어요.
I was driving when a cat suddenly
jumped into the road.

"깜짝 놀랐어요"

길을 걷고 있는데 차 한 대가 갑자기
내 뒤에서 경적을 울렸어.
I was walking down the street, and
a car suddenly honked behind me!

"깜짝 놀랐어"

교실에서 혼자 생각에 잠겨 있을 때,
갑자기 누군가가 문을 열었어요.
When I was lost in thought alone
in the classroom, someone suddenly
opened the door.

"깜짝이야! 놀랐어"

한밤중에 호텔에 화재 경보가 울려서
모두 대피했지만 오작동으로 밝혀졌어요.
A fire alarm went off at the hotel in
the middle of the night and everyone
evacuated, but it turned out to be a
false alarm.

"깜짝 놀랐어요"

우리 아들이 자다가 갑자기 소리를 질렀어.
My son suddenly screamed while sleeping.

"깜짝 놀랐어"

신기하다

[신기하다] [singihada]

* 1. 믿을 수 없을 정도로 색다르고 이상하다.

Unbelievably unusual and strange.

* 2. 처음 보는 것이어서 새롭고 이상하다.

New and stange because one has never seen it before.

●

신기해

[신기해] [singihae]

신기해요

[신기해요] [singihaeyo]

●

해외여행은 그때가 처음이라 모든 것이
새롭고 궁금했어요.
That was my first overseas trip and
everything made me wonder.

"신기해요"

로봇 요리사가 만든 버거를 먹어 봤는데,
맛있었어.
I have tried a burger made by a robot
cook, and it was good.

"신기해"

어린아이들이 말을 배우는 것은 정말 놀라워.
It's truly amazing how small children
pick up words.

"신기해"

마술사는 반지를 상자 안에 넣고 불을 붙였고,
토끼 한 마리가 상자 밖으로 나왔어요.
The magician put the ring in the box and
lit it, and a rabbit came out of the box.

"신기해요"

동물들은 지진이나 화산 폭발 같은 자연재해를
먼저 예측하고 미리 대피해요.
Animals predict natural disasters such as
earthquakes and volcanic eruptions first
and evacuate in advance.

"신기해요"

신나다

[신나다] [sinnada]

* 흥이 나고 기분이 아주 좋아지다.

To get excited and come to feel very good.

신나

[신나] [sinna]

신나요

[신나요] [sinnayo]

불금이다!
오늘 퇴근하고 친구들이랑 파티에 갈 거야.
TGIF!
I'm going to a party with my friends
after work today.

"신나"

우리는 내일 디즈니랜드에 갈 거예요.
We're going to Disneyland tomorrow.

"신나요"

한국 여행은 처음이라 최대한 알차게
다녀올 거야.
It's my first trip to Korea,
so I'm going to make the most of it.

"신나"

우리 아이들은 크리스마스 선물을 뜯느라
바빠.
My children are busy opening their
presents for Christmas.

"신나"

우리 부서는 이번 달에 특별 보너스를 받아.
My department receives a special bonus
this month.

"신나"

짜릿하다

[짜리타다] [jjaritada]

* 심리적 자극을 받아 마음이 순간적으로 조금 흥분되고 떨리는 듯하다.
Feeling slightly excited and tense temporarily out of a psychological stimulation.

짜릿해

[짜리태] [jjaritae]

짜릿해요

[짜리태요] [jjaritaeyo]

그는 하프 타임 직전에 역전골을 넣었어요.

He scored a tie-breaking goal just
before halftime.

"짜릿해요"

놀이공원에서 친구들과 롤러코스터를 탔어.

와! 이 롤러코스터 진짜 재미있다!

I rode a roller coaster at the theme park
with my friends.

Wow! This roller coaster is really fun!

"짜릿해"

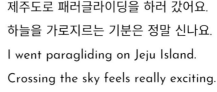

제주도로 패러글라이딩을 하러 갔어요.

하늘을 가로지르는 기분은 정말 신나요.

I went paragliding on Jeju Island.

Crossing the sky feels really exciting.

"짜릿해요"

내가 좋아하는 가수의 공연을 직접 보러 갔어.

그 가수의 노래를 직접 듣다니 믿을 수가 없어.

I went to see my favorite singer's performance
in person.

I can't believe I'm hearing his song firsthand.

"짜릿해"

해변에서 서프보드에 올라서는 연습을 수없이
한 후에, 마침내 바다에 들어가 서프보드 위에
설 수 있었어.

I practiced how to pop up on the surfboard
countless times on the beach. I was finally able
to enter the sea and stand on the surfboard.

"짜릿해"

당황스럽다

[당황스럽따] [danghwangseureoptta]

* 놀라거나 매우 급하여 어떻게 해야 할지를 모르는 데가 있다.

Not knowing what to do because one is caught off guard or in a big
hurry.

●

당황스러워

[당황스러워] [danghwangseureowo]

당황스러워요

[당황스러워요] [danghwangseureowoyo]

●

◎ -스럽다 [쓰럽따] [seureoptta]

명사 뒤에 붙어 '그러한 성질이 있음'의 뜻을 더하고 형용사로 만드는 단어.

This word is attached after a noun and adds the meaning of 'having
such attributes' so that the noun becomes an adjective.

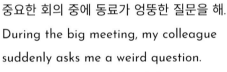

수업 시간에 딴 생각을 하고 있는데
갑자기 선생님께서 질문을 하셨어요.
I was thinking about something else
during class, and the teacher asked
me a question out of the blue.
"당황스러워요"

마트에서 물건을 사서 계산하려고 했는데
지갑을 안 가져온 걸 알았어.
I was going to buy something at the
mart and pay for it, but I realized
I didn't bring my wallet.
"당황스러워"

중요한 회의 중에 동료가 엉뚱한 질문을 해.
During the big meeting, my colleague
suddenly asks me a weird question.
"당황스러워"

요즘 다이어트 중이라 많이 못 먹었는데
오늘 아침에 몸무게를 쟀더니 살이 더 쪘어.
I haven't eaten much lately because I'm on
a diet. But I weighed myself this morning
and found that I gained more weight.
"당황스러워"

내 여자 친구가 물어봐요.
"나 뭐 달라진 것 없어?"
My girlfriend asks me.
"Do you notice anything different about me?"
'당황스러워'

기겁하다

[기거파다] [gigeopada]

* 숨이 막힐 듯이 갑자기 놀라거나 겁에 질리다.

To suddenly be surprised or frightened by something.

●

기겁했어

[기거패써] [gigeopaesseo]

기겁했어요

[기거패써요] [gigeopaesseoyo]

●

어제 내 여자친구랑 클럽에서 마주쳤어.

I bumped into my girlfriend in the club
last night.

"기겁했어"

새 아이폰을 사서 매장에서 나오다가
실수로 떨어뜨렸어.

I bought a new iPhone but accidentally
dropped it while leaving the store.

"기겁했어"

씻으려고 욕실 불을 켰는데 바퀴벌레가
날아다니고 있었어요.

I turned on the bathroom light to wash
up, but a cockroach was flying around.

"기겁했어요"

하루 종일 컴퓨터 앞에 앉아서 서류 작업을
했어. 그런데 실수로 삭제 버튼을 눌렀어.

I sat in front of the computer all day
working on paperwork.

However, I accidentally pressed the
delete button.

"기겁했어"

내 친구가 암에 걸렸다고 나한테 거짓말했을 때
드는 마음.

This is how I felt when my friend lied to me
that he got cancer.

"기겁했어요"

얼떨떨하다

[얼떨떨하다] [eoltteoltteolhada]

* 1. 뜻밖의 일로 당황하거나 여러 가지 일이 복잡하여 어찌할 바를 모르는 데가 있다.
Embarrassed about an unexpected thing or not knowing what to do due to several complex things.
* 2. 머리가 심하게 울리고 어지럽다.
Feeling dizzy and like one has a heavy pounding in one's head.

얼떨떨해

[얼떨떨해] [eoltteoltteolhae]

얼떨떨해요

[얼떨떨해요] [eoltteoltteolhaeyo]

개의 갑작스러운 기분 변화에 완전히
어리둥절했어.
I was totally bewildered by his sudden
change of mood.

"얼떨떨해"

나에겐 오래된 친구가 있어. 하지만 걔는
갑자기 날 오랫동안 좋아했다고 고백했어.
I have an old friend. But he suddenly
confessed that he had liked me for a long
time.

"얼떨떨해"

선생님께선 내가 졸업식에서 상을 받을 거라고
말씀하셨어. 상을 받을 거라고는 상상도 못했어.
The teacher told me that I would win an
award at the graduation ceremony.
I never expected that I would win an award.

"얼떨떨해"

내 노래가 많은 사람들의 관심을 받고 있어요.
이런 관심을 받은 적은 난생처음이에요.
My song is getting a lot of attention. I've
never received such attention ever in my life.

"얼떨떨해요"

우리 딸이 수능시험에서 만점을 받았다니
믿어지지 않아.
I can't believe my daughter got a perfect
score on the College Scholastic Ability Test.

"얼떨떨해"

헷갈리다

[헫깔리다] [hetkkallida]

동의어 (synonym) = 헛갈리다 [헏깔리다] [heotkkallida]

* 1. 정신이 어지럽고 혼란스럽게 되다.

To feel dizzy and confused.

* 2. 여러 가지가 뒤섞여 일의 방향을 잡지 못하다.

To fail to set a direction of a task as many things are mixed up.

●

헷갈려

[헫깔려] [hetkkallyeo]

헷갈려요

[헫깔려요] [hetkkallyeoyo]

●

가구를 샀는데 설명서를 봐도 어떻게
조립해야 할지 모르겠어요.
I bought furniture, but I don't know
how to put it together even when
reading the instructions.

"헷갈려요"

뭐야? 그러니까 넌 걔가 그렇게 하는 게
좋다는 거야? 싫다는 거야?
What? So do you mean that
you like him to do that or not?

"헷갈려"

한국어 '빵'과 '방'은 비슷하게 들리지
않나요?
Doesn't the Korean word '빵' sound
similar to the Korean word '방'?

"헷갈려요"

걔는 나한테 관심도 없다면서 왜 자꾸
날 보고 웃지?
She said she wasn't interested in me,
so why does she keep smiling at me?

"헷갈려"

그 쌍둥이는 너무 비슷해서 누가 누군지
구별할 수가 없어.
The twins are so alike I can't tell which
is which.

"헷갈려"

한심하다

[한심하다] [hansimhada]

* 정도에 너무 지나치거나 모자라서 딱하거나 어이없다.

Looking pitiable or making another dumbfounded because one goes

far beyond a certain limit or falls short of his/her expectation.

●

한심해

[한심해] [hansimhae]

한심해요

[한심해요] [hansimhaeyo]

●

다이어트는 작심삼일로 끝났어.
I couldn't stick to my resolutions
of going on a diet.

"한심해"

걘 돈 좀 있다고 흥청망청 쓰더니 결국
하는 사업마다 다 망했어.
He spent a lot of money recklessly and
eventually ruined every business he tried.

"한심해"

걘 미국의 명문 대학교를 졸업했는데
집에서 아무것도 안 하고 놀고 있어.
She graduated from one of the most
prestigious universities in the US,
but she's sitting at home doing nothing.

"한심해"

그게 문제가 될 거라고 미리 경고했었어.
그런데 넌 지금 전문적인 지식도 없이
뭘 해야 할지 막막해하고 있어.
I warned you beforehand that it would be a
problem for you. But now you are clueless as
to what to do, with no expertise.

"한심해"

걘 자기가 무슨 짓을 했는지도 모르고 웃고 있어.
He's smiling without even being aware of
what he has done.

"한심해"

어이없다

[어이업따] [eoieoptta]

동의어 (synonym) = 어처구니없다 [어처구니업따][eocheogunieoptta]

* 너무 뜻밖의 일을 당해서 기가 막히는 듯하다.

Being dumbfounded due to an extremely unexpected occurrence.

●

어이없어

[어이업써] [eoieopsseo]

어이없어요

[어이업써요] [eoieopsseoyo]

●

◎ '어처구니'는 맷돌의 손잡이를 가리키는 말입니다.

맷돌을 돌리려고 하는데 손잡이가 없다고 생각해 보세요. 너무 황당하겠죠?

'어처구니' refers to the handle of a millstone.

Imagine you're trying to turn a millstone, but there's no handle.

That must be ridiculous, right?

우린 그냥 널 도와주려고 온 거야.
우리한테 화풀이하지 마.
We're just here to help you.
Don't take it out on us.
"어이없어"

내가 네 부탁을 들어주고 있는 거야.
그 반대가 아니라.
I'm doing you a favor, not vice versa.
"어이없어"

넌 내 호의를 당연하게 생각하는구나.
You're taking me for granted.
"어이없어"

왜 소리 질러?
널 보러 온 건 나밖에 없는데. 니가 망쳤잖아!
Why are you yelling at me?
I'm the only one here. You ruined it!
"어이없어"

주말 내내 너를 위해 처음부터 직접 만들었어!
최소한 마음에 드는 척이라도 할 수 있잖아.
I made it from scratch for you all weekend!
You could at least pretend to like it.
"어이없어"

충격적

[충격쩍] [chunggyeokjjeok]

충격적 + 이다 = 충격적이다 [충격쩍이다] [chunggyeokjjeogida]

* 정신적으로 충격을 받을 만한 것.

The state of something causing a mental shock.

충격적이야

[충격적이야] [chunggyeokjjeogiya]

충격적이에요

[충격적이에요] [chunggyeokjjeogieyo]

◎ 충격 [충격] [chunggyeok]

* 슬픈 일이나 뜻밖의 사건 등으로 마음에 받은 심한 자극이나 영향.

A very strong stimulation or influence one receives from a sad incident or an unexpected accident, etc.

◎ -적 [-적] [-jeok]

* '그 성격을 띠는', '그에 관계된', '그 상태로 된'의 뜻을 더하는 접미사.

A suffix used to mean 'having that character,' 'being related to something,' 'being such a state.'

엊그제까지만 해도 괜찮았던 그가 죽었다니
믿을 수 없어!
I can't believe he's dead!
He was fine just the other day!
"충격적이야"

동물들이 고통스러워하는 것을 사람들이
보고 즐긴다는 게 믿어지지 않아.
I can't believe people enjoyed watching
the animals suffer.
"충격적이야"

이 영화는 실제로 일어났던 엽기적인 연쇄 살인
사건을 바탕으로 만들어졌어.
실제로 이런 일이 있었다니 믿을 수 없어.
This movie is based on a grotesque serial
murder case that actually took place.
I can't believe this actually happened!
"충격적이야"

한국에 온 외국인들이 카페에 노트북과 가방을 두고
화장실에 가는 한국인을 볼 때 드는 마음.
This is how foreigners feel when they come to
Korea and see Koreans going to the restroom
leaving their laptops and bags at cafes.
"충격적이에요" (Culture shock)

그것은 정치인들이 국민들을 상대로 저지른 가장 큰
사기 행각으로 드러났어요.
It turned out to be the biggest fraud politicians
have committed against the people.
"충격적이에요"

두려움

FEAR

허무하다

[허무하다] [heomuhada]

* 가치 없고 의미 없게 느껴져 매우 허전하고 쓸쓸하다.

Thinking of something as worthless and meaningless, making one feel extremely empty and lonely.

●

허무해

[허무해] [heomuhae]

허무해요

[허무해요] [heomuhaeyo]

●

코로나 때문에 내가 아무것도 하지 않는 동안
일 년이 지나버렸어.
Because of COVID-19, a year has just
passed while I was doing nothing.

"허무해"

우린 소문난 맛집을 찾아서 가려고 했는데
하필 오늘 쉬는 날이래요.
We found a famous restaurant by word of
mouth, so we planned to go there today,
but they say it's closed today.

"허무해요"

그 계약을 따내려고 노력했지만 아무 성과 없이
끝났어.
I tried to win the contract, but it ended
without any results.

"허무해"

난 벌써 짐을 다 쌌는데 비 때문에 캠프 여행이
취소되었어.
I've already packed. However, my camping
trip got rained out.

"허무해"

몇 주 동안 열심히 일했는데 노트북이 고장 나서
자료가 모두 날아가 버렸어.
모든 노력이 헛수고가 되었어.
I've been working hard for weeks, but my
laptop broke down and all the data are gone.
All my hard work went to waste.

"허무해"

주눅 들다

[주ː눅 들다] [juːnuk deulda]

주눅 + 들다 = 주눅 들다

(사람이) 무섭거나 부끄러워 기세가 약해지다.

Feeling intimidated due to being scared of
or embarrassed before a person.

주눅 들어

[주ː눅 드러] [juːnuk deureo]

주눅 들어요

[주ː눅 드러요] [juːnuk deureoyo]

◎ 주눅 [주ː눅] [juːnuk]

* 기를 펴지 못하고 움츠러드는 태도.

An attitude of lacking confidence and shying away.

◎ 들다 [들다] [deulda]

* 어떤 것에 대한 생각이나 느낌이 생기다.

For an opinion or feeling to arise toward a certain thing.

독설가인 상사 앞에만 서면 난 위축돼서
입도 뻥긋 못해요.
Every time I face my boss, who is
a spiteful critic, I get daunted and
can't even open my mouth.
"주눅 들어요"

다른 사람들 앞에서 발표할 때 너무 소심해져.
I become so timid when making a
presentation in front of others.
"주눅 들어"

파티에 온 모든 여자들은 화려했는데,
거울에 비친 나는 너무 초라해 보여.
All the girls at the party were gorgeous,
but my reflection in the mirror looked so
shabby.
"주눅 들어"

부유한 사람들에게서 풍기는 느긋하고도
넉넉한 분위기에 나는 아무 말도 하지 못했어요.
I remained silent and still in the relaxed and
generous atmosphere of the wealthy people.
"주눅 들어요"

난 뭐든지 잘하는 형 때문에 자신감 없이 자랐어.
I grew up without confidence because of
my older brother who excels at everything.
"주눅 들어"

무섭다

[무섭따] [museoptta]

* 어떤 대상이 꺼려지거나 무슨 일이 일어날까 두렵다.
Feeling scared of something,
or feeling afraid something might happen.

●

무서워

[무서워] [museowo]

무서워요

[무서워요] [museowoyo]

●

난 겁이 많아. 그래서 혼자 자는 걸 안 좋아해.

I'm easily frightened.

So I don't like sleeping alone.

"무서워"

공포영화를 보고 있는데 방문이 흔들려요.

I'm watching a horror movie and the door
is shaking.

"무서워요"

걔는 항상 진짜 착하고 조용해요.

온순한 사람이 화내니까 너무 놀랐어요.

She's always super nice and quiet. I was so
surprised to see a meek person get mad.

"무서워요"

어렸을 때 개한테 물려서 개를 좋아하지 않아.

길에서 개 한 마리가 나한테 다가와.

I don't like dogs because I was bitten by dogs
when I was little.

A dog approaches me on the street.

"무서워요"

요즘 흉악한 범죄가 많이 일어나서 나는 밤에 혼자
나갈 때 항상 조심해요.

There are a lot of violent crimes these days, so
I'm always careful when I go out alone at night.

"무서워요"

지하실에 혼자 내려갈 때마다 뭔가 튀어나올 것 같아.

Whenever I go down to the basement alone,
I feel like something is going to pop out.

"무서워"

두렵다

[두렵따] [duryeoptta]

* 1. 몹시 피하고 싶을 만큼 겁이 나고 무섭다.
So afraid and frightened as to feel like avoiding
something or someone.
* 2. 걱정되고 불안하다.
Feeling anxious and uneasy.

●

두려워

[두려워] [duryeowo]

두려워요

[두려워요] [duryeowoyo]

●

주식 시장이 폭락하고 있어요!

The stock market is crashing!

"두려워요"

나이가 많아서 새로운 일을 시작하려고
할 때마다 망설여져.

I hesitate whenever I try to start
a new job because I'm old.

"두려워"

내일 암을 제거하는 수술을 받아야 해.

I have to undergo an operation
to remove cancer tomorrow.

"두려워"

나는 고소 공포증이 있어서 높은 곳에
올라가는 것이 겁나.

Since I have acrophobia, I'm afraid
of going up to high places.

"두려워"

코로나 바이러스는 전염성이 매우 강해서
많은 사람들이 걱정을 하고 있어요.

There's a lot of anxiety going around
because coronavirus is very contagious.

"두려워요"

밤에 집으로 걸어가는데 낯선 사람이 계속
내 뒤를 따라왔어요.

I was walking home at night,
and a stranger kept following me.

"두려워요"

조마조마하다

[조마조마하다] [jomajomahada]

* 앞으로 닥칠 일이 걱정되어 마음이 초조하고 불안하다.

Anxious and uneasy for fear of things to come.

●

조마조마해

[조마조마해] [jomajomahae]

조마조마해요

[조마조마해요] [jomajomahaeyo]

●

난 합격자 발표를 기다리고 있어요.

I'm waiting for the announcement of
successful applicants.

"조마조마해요"

엄마한테 거짓말한 것이 들통날까 봐
가슴이 두근거렸어.

My heart was pounding because I feared
I'd be caught lying to my mom.

"조마조마해"

나는 밤늦게 들어온 것을 부모님께 들킬까 봐
살금살금 방으로 들어갔어.

I tiptoed into my room so my parents
wouldn't catch me coming back home late.

"조마조마해"

달고나¹ 뽑기를 할 때 모양이 깨질까 봐 긴장돼.

I'm nervous that I might break the shape
when I carve out dalgona.

"조마조마해"

공항으로 가는 중인데 차가 너무 막혀.
비행기를 놓치면 어쩌지?

I'm on my way to the airport, but the traffic
is jammed. What if I miss the plane?

"조마조마해"

곡예사가 외줄을 따라 걸어가자 관객들은
숨을 죽이고 지켜보았어요.

As the acrobat walked along the single line,
the audience watched him breathlessly.

"조마조마해요"

---

1. 달고나 : 달고나는 설탕을 녹여 식소다를 섞은 후 그것을 납작하게 해서 여러 가지 모양을 찍은 것입니다.

Dalgona is made by melting sugar, mixing it with soda, flattening it, and molding it into various shapes.

긴장되다

[긴장되다/긴장뒈다] [ginjangdoeda/ginjangdweda]

* 1. 마음을 놓지 못하고 정신을 바짝 차리게 되다.

To be alerted, not being relaxed.

* 2. 서로의 관계가 평온하지 않고 다툼이 일어날 듯하게 되다.

For a relationship to become disturbed

and seem as if a dispute is about to happen.

●

긴장돼

[긴장돼:] [ginjangdwae:]

긴장돼요

[긴장돼:요] [ginjangdwae:yo]

●

중요한 발표가 있어서 밤새 잠을 설쳤어.
I had an important presentation,
so I couldn't sleep all night.
"긴장돼"

반지를 준비했어. 오늘 저녁 식사 후
내 여자친구에게 청혼할 거야.
I prepared a ring. I'm going to propose
to my girlfriend after dinner tonight.
"긴장돼"

오늘 처음으로 고속도로에서 운전을 해요.
손에 땀이 자꾸 나요.
I'm driving on the highway for the first time
today. My hands are sweating endlessly.
"긴장돼요"

내일 시험이 있어요. 만약에 또 시험에서 떨어지면,
마지막 승진 기회는 없어질 거예요.
I have a test tomorrow. If I fail the test again,
my last promotion opportunity will be gone.
"긴장돼요"

걔네들은 항상 서로 대립하고, 어떤 것에도 의견이
일치하지 않아.
그래서 같이 있으면 무슨 일이 생길 것 같아.
They're always at odds with each other and
they never agree on anything. So I think
something will happen when I'm with them.
"긴장돼"

초조하다

[초조하다] [chojohada]

* 답답하거나 안타깝거나 걱정이 되어 마음이 조마조마하다.

Feeling uneasy because one is stifled, sorry, or worried.

●

초초해

[초조해] [chojohae]

초초해요

[초조해요] [chojohaeyo]

●

우리 엄마는 아직도 수술 중이고,
우린 아직 아무 말도 듣지 못했어.
My mom is still in surgery and
we haven't heard any news yet.
"초조해"

면접이 있어서 내 차례를 기다리고 있어.
I have an interview, so I'm waiting
for my turn.
"초조해"

운전면허 시험을 보는데 자꾸 시동이 꺼져요.
I'm taking the driver's license test,
but the engine keeps turning off.
"초조해요"

갠 의사가 검사 결과를 전화로 알려주기로
해서 기다리는 중이야. 그래서 하루 종일
가만히 있지를 못하고 있어.
He's waiting for the doctor to call with
the test results. So he's been like a cat
on hot bricks all day.
"초조해"

우린 오늘 첫 공연이 있어요.
가슴과 등에 땀을 비 오듯이 흘렸어요.
We have our first performance today. We
sweated like rain on my back and chest.
"초조해요"

불편하다

[불편하다] [bulpyeonhada]

* 1. 몸이나 마음이 편하지 않고 괴롭다.

The body or mind being uncomfortable and painful.

* 2. 다른 사람과의 관계 등이 편하지 않다.

The relationship with another person, etc., being awkward.

●

불편해

[불편해] [bulpyeonhae]

불편해요

[불편해요] [bulpyeonhaeyo]

●

해야 할 일을 다 안 하고 퇴근해버렸어.
I left work without doing everything
I had to do.

"불편해"

그 일이 있고 나서, 우리는 좀 어색해졌어요.
After what had happened, things
became a bit awkward between us.

"불편해요"

새 신발이 발에 너무 꽉 껴서 발이 아파 죽겠어.
These new shoes are so tight that my feet
are killing me.

"불편해"

화가 나서 친구에게 안 좋은 말을 하기는 했지
만, 그 뒤로 계속 마음이 좋지 않아요.
I said bad things to my friend because I
was angry, but I didn't feel good ever since.

"불편해요"

내 친구의 남편이 다른 여자와 바람을 피우는
걸 봤어. 하지만 내 친구에게 말할 수 없었어.
다 알고도 모른 척하는 게 답답해.
I saw my friend's husband cheating with
another woman. But I couldn't tell my
friend. It's frustrating to pretend you don't
know even though you know everything.

"불편해"

불안하다

[부란하다] [buranhada]

* 마음이 편하지 않고 조마조마하다.

Being anxious without feeling at ease.

●

불안해

[부란해] [buranhae]

불안해요

[부란해요] [buranhaeyo]

●

뭔가 안 좋은 예감이 들어.

I get a bad feeling about this.

"불안해"

난기류 때문에 비행기가 계속 흔들려요.

The plane keeps shaking because of turbulence.

"불안해요"

나 걔한테 거짓말했어. 들키면 어쩌지?

I lied to her. What if I get caught?

"불안해"

여진은 하루 종일 계속되었어요.

Aftershocks continued throughout the day.

"불안해요"

불특정 다수를 겨냥한 테러가 곳곳에서 일어나고 있어요.

Terrorist attacks targeted at random people are occurring here and there.

"불안해요"

우리 회사가 경영난으로 문을 닫을지도 모른다는 소문이 있어.

There are rumors that my company may be closed because of financial difficulties.

"불안해"

걱정되다

[걱쩡되다/걱쩡뒈다]

[geokjjeongdoeda/geokjjeongdweda]

* 좋지 않은 일이 있을까 봐 두렵고 불안한 마음이 들다.

To become fearful and anxious that something bad might happen.

●

걱정돼

[걱쩡돼ː] [geokjjeongdwaeː]

걱정돼요

[걱쩡돼ː요] [geokjjeongdwaeːyo]

●

우리 부모님께서는 COVID-19에 걸리셨어요.
밤새 열이 나고 목이 너무 아프시대요.
My parents got COVID-19. They had a fever
all night and their throats hurt so much.

"걱정돼요"

내 가장 친한 친구는 여자친구와 헤어진 후
일주일 내내 술을 마시고 있어.
My best friend has been drinking all week
since he broke up with his girlfriend.

"걱정돼"

우리 아들은 혼자 해외 유학을 갔어요.
그래서 밥은 잘 챙겨 먹고 다니는지, 아프지는
않은지 자주 전화를 해요.
My son went abroad to study alone.
So I call him often to see if he eats well or
whether he isn't sick.

"걱정돼요"

내일 캠핑 가는데 아까부터 비가 와. 일기 예보에서
밤새 비가 올 거래. 내일 출발할 수 있을까?
I'm going camping tomorrow, but it's been
raining since earlier. According to the weather
forecast, it will rain all night.
Will I be able to set off tomorrow?

"걱정돼"

우리 남편이 너무 열심히 일해서 건강을 해칠 것 같아.
My husband is working so hard that I think it's
going to ruin his health.

"걱정돼"

심란하다

[심난하다] [simnanhada]

* 마음이 편안하지 못하고 어지럽다.

Feeling uncomfortable and confused.

●

심란해

[심난해] [simnanhae]

심란해요

[심난해요] [simnanhaeyo]

●

◎ 심난하다 [심:난하다] [sim:nanhada]  vs 심란하다

'심난하다'는 형편이나 처지 등이 매우 어렵다는 뜻이고,

'심란하다'는 마음이 어수선하다는 뜻입니다.

따라서 '마음이 심란하다'로 쓰는 것이 알맞습니다.

'심난하다' means that circumstances are very difficult and

'심란하다' means that the mind is troubled.

Therefore, it is appropriate to write "my mind is 심란하다."

우리 딸은 너무 철이 없어서 걔를 볼 때마다
한숨이 나와.
My daughter is so immature that I sigh
whenever I see her.

"심란해"

내 월급 빼고 다 올랐어요.
물가가 정말 많이 올랐어요.
Everything except for my income has been
raised. The price has gone up really high.

"심란해요"

금요일에 체조 대회가 있어요.
하지만 안타깝게도 발목 부상을 당했어요.
There's a gymnastics competition on Friday.
But unfortunately, I injured my ankles.

"심란해요"

요즘 몸이 안 좋아서 병원에 갔는데 의사 선생님이
서울에 있는 큰 병원으로 가보라고 했어.
I haven't been in good health these days,
so I went to the doctor but she told me I
should go to a bigger hospital in Seoul.

"심란해"

이번에 등록금이 또 올라서 열심히 아르바이트를 해서
학비를 모으고 있는데, 오늘 아르바이트에서 잘렸어.
My tuition has gone up again this time.
That's why I'm saving money by working hard
part-time to pay for my tuition, but I got fired
from my part-time job today.

"심란해"

부담스럽다

[부ː담스럽따] [buːdamseureoptta]

* 어떤 일이나 상황이 감당하기 어려운 느낌이 있다.

A matter or situation being difficult to handle.

●

부담스러워

[부ː담스러워] [buːdamseureowo]

부담스러워요

[부ː담스러워요] [buːdamseureowoyo]

●

◎ -스럽다 [쓰럽따] [seureoptta]

명사 뒤에 붙어 '그러한 성질이 있음'의 뜻을 더하고, 형용사로 만드는 단어.

This word is attached after a noun and adds the meaning of 'having

such attributes' so that the noun becomes an adjective.

차는 마음에 드는데 가격이 너무 비싸.

I like this car, but the price is too high.

"부담스러워"

개가 내 생일선물로 비싼 가방을 사주겠데요.

He said he would buy me an expensive
bag for my birthday.

"부담스러워요"

개가 내 눈을 똑바로 쳐다보면서
"난 널 사랑해"라고 했어.

난 걔를 안지 3 일밖에 안됐어.

He was staring right into my eyes saying
"I'm in love with you."

I've only known him for three days.

"부담스러워"

걘 항상 잘 차려입어.

그런데 가끔 너무 과하게 느껴져.

She always dresses up.

But It feels too much at times.

"부담스러워"

프레젠테이션을 준비하고 있었어요.

사장님께서 "내일 프레젠테이션 기대할게요"
라고 말씀하셨어요.

I was preparing for my presentation.

My boss said, "I'll anticipate your
presentation tomorrow."

"부담스러워요"

버겁다

[버겁따] [beogeoptta]

* 어떤 일을 하거나 살아가는 데 능력이 미치지 못해 힘들다.

Having difficulty in doing something or making a living due to lack of ability.

●

버거워

[버거워] [beogeowo]

버거워요

[버거워요] [beogeowoyo]

●

◎ 벅차다 vs 버겁다

'벅차다'는 긍정적일 때도 사용할 수 있지만 '버겁다'는 부정적일 때만 사용한다.

'벅차다' can also be used for positive matters, but '버겁다' is used only for negative matters.

이 아파트는 너무 커서 유지비가 많이 들어.
This apartment is so big that it costs
a lot to maintain it.
"버거워"

이 건물에는 엘리베이터가 없는데
옮길 짐이 너무 많아요.
This building has no elevator,
but I have too much luggage to carry.
"버거워요"

로봇을 이용하는 프로젝트를 하고 있어요.
그런데 로봇에 대한 배경지식이 전혀 없어서
너무 힘들어요.
I'm working on a project using robots.
But I have no background knowledge of
robots, so it's very difficult.
"버거워요"

요즘 일이 너무 많아서 회사에서 스트레스를
많이 받았어. 진짜 스트레스를 감당할 수가 없어.
I've been under a lot of stress at work lately
due to a heavy workload.
I literally cannot handle the stress.
"버거워"

일하면서 아이 셋 키우는 것은 너무 힘들어.
It's hard juggling work and raising three kids.
"버거워"

슬픔

SADNESS

후회되다

[후ː회되다/후ː훼뒈다] [huːhoedoeda/huːhwedweda]

* 이전에 자신이 한 일이 잘못임이 깨달아지고
스스로 자신의 잘못을 나무라게 되다.

To come to realize that what one did was wrong

and reprimand oneself for having done it.

●

후회돼

[후ː회돼ː] [huːhoedwaeː]

후회돼요

[후ː회되요] [huːhoedwaeːyo]

●

주가가 폭등했어요.

그때 그 주식을 샀어야 했는데!

The stock prices spiked.

I should have bought that stock then!

"후회돼요"

난 불평만 하고 걔들을 이해하려고

노력하지 않았어.

I only complained and didn't try to

understand them.

"후회돼"

화가 나서 나도 모르게 걔한테 나쁜 말을 불쑥

내뱉었어. 내 모진 말이 걔한테 깊은 상처를 줬어.

I got angry and blurted out bad words to

her in spite of myself.

My cruel remarks deeply wounded her.

"후회돼"

내 전 남자친구는 좋은 사람이었어.

근데 왜 걔랑 헤어졌는지 나도 모르겠어.

그런 사람을 다시는 만나지 못할까 봐 두려워.

My ex-boyfriend was a great guy.

But I don't know why I broke up with him.

I'm afraid I'm never going to meet someone

like him again.

"후회돼"

진짜 돈 하나도 없어. 충동구매 그만해야지.

I'm literally penniless. No more impulse buying.

"후회돼"

부끄럽다

[부끄럽따] [bukkeureoptta]

* 1. 쑥스럽거나 수줍다

Bashful or coy.

* 2. 창피하거나 떳떳하지 못하다.

Feeling shame with an uneasy conscience.

●

부끄러워

[부끄러워] [bukkeureowo]

부끄러워요

[부끄러워요] [bukkeureowoyo]

●

내가 짝사랑하던 여자가 말을 걸어왔어.
내 얼굴은 홍당무처럼 빨개졌어.
The girl I had a crush on talked to me.
My face turned red like a carrot.
"부끄러워"

거짓말이 들통나서 걔를 쳐다볼 수가 없었어.
I couldn't look at her because I was
caught lying.
"부끄러워"

제가 계속 일을 미뤄서 우리 팀 전체에
상당한 피해를 줬어요.
I kept procrastinating and ended up
severely damaging the whole team.
"부끄러워요"

이렇게 칭찬해 주시니 몸 둘 바를 모르겠네요.
비행기 그만 태워요!
I don't know how to react to your words of
praise. Stop sweet talking!
"부끄러워요"

그러지 말았어야 했는데. 어렸을 때
내 친구에게 상처 준 것을 후회해.
I shouldn't have done that. I regret doing
things that hurt my friend when I was little.
"부끄러워"

난 조용하고 수줍음이 많은 성격이라서
많은 사람들 앞에서 노래 부르는 것이 쉽지 않아.
I'm quiet and shy, so it's not easy for me to
sing in front of hundreds of people.
"부끄러워"

창피하다

[창피하다] [changpihada]

* 체면이 깎이는 어떤 일이나 사실 때문에 몹시 부끄럽다.
Being very ashamed due to a disgraceful event or fact.

●

창피해

[창피해] [changpihae]

창피해요

[창피해요] [changpihaeyo]

●

많은 사람들 앞에서 넘어졌을 때 드는 마음.
This is how I felt when I fell down in
front of many people.

"창피해"

가: 너 남대문 열렸어!
나: 맙소사, 그래서 사람들이 나를 쳐다봤구나!

A: Your fly is open!
B: Oh my gosh, that's why people were
looking at me!

"창피해"

내가 엘리베이터에서 방귀를 뀌자 엘리베이터
에 있던 모든 사람들이 코를 막았어요.

When I farted in the elevator,
everyone in there held their noses.

"창피해요"

난 성공하기 위해 비겁한 짓을 서슴없이 했었
어. 그땐 내가 왜 그랬을까?

I didn't hesitate to hit below the belt to
be successful.
Why did I do that back then?

"창피해"

공공장소에서 내 친구는 내 옆에 앉아서
큰소리로 통화를 했어.
In a public place, my friend was sitting next
to me and talking loudly on his cell phone.

"창피해"

따분하다

[따분하다] [ttabunhada]

* 재미가 없어 지루하고 답답하다.

Uninteresting, tedious, and stodgy.

따분해

[따분해] [ttabunhae]

따분해요

[따분해요] [ttabunhaeyo]

교수님께선 제가 이해하지 못하는 것을
계속 말씀하셨어요.
The professor kept talking about things
I didn't understand.

"따분해요"

난 만날 친구도 없고 할 일도 없어서
주말 내내 집에서 빈둥거렸어.
I didn't have any friends or anything to do,
so I spent all weekend hanging around at
home.

"따분해"

특별한 일 없이 매일 반복되는 똑같은 일상이야.
The same routine repeats every day
without anything special.

"따분해"

이 세미나는 무슨 말을 하는지도 모르겠고
무진장 길어! 나 심지어 세미나 중에 졸았어.
I don't know what this seminar is about,
and it's very long! I even dozed off during
the seminar.

"따분해"

우리 사장님은 식상한 이야기를 아침마다 하세요.
그런데 전부 아재 개그라서 재미있지도 않아요.
My boss talks cliché every morning.
But everything he says is an old man's joke,
so it's not even funny.

"따분해요"

쓸쓸하다

[쓸쓸하다] [sseulsseulhada]

* 마음이 외롭고 허전하다.
Feeling lonely and empty.

●

쓸쓸해

[쓸쓸해] [sseulsseulhae]

쓸쓸해요

[쓸쓸해요] [sseulsseulhaeyo]

●

오늘 내 생일인데 아무도 내 생일인 지
몰라서 혼자 보냈어.
It's my birthday today, but no one knew
it was my birthday, so I spent it alone.

"쓸쓸해"

우리 부모님께선 저와 자주 소통하지
않으셔서 전 너무 외로웠어요.
My parents don't communicate with me
often, so I was very lonely.

"쓸쓸해요"

이 도시로 이사 온 지 얼마 안 돼서
아는 사람이 한 명도 없어.
I just moved to this city, so I don't know
anyone.

"쓸쓸해"

날씨가 점점 추워져서 단풍도 다 떨어지고
겨울 산에 등산가는 사람도 거의 없어요.
It's getting colder and colder, so the autumn
leaves are all gone, and there are few hikers
in the wintertime mountains.

"쓸쓸해요"

오랜만에 고향에 왔어. 고향은 예전 모습
그대로인데, 마중 나올 친구가 한 명도 없어.
It's been a long time since I came to my hometown. My hometown is the same as before,
but I don't have any friends to greet me.

"쓸쓸해"

허전하다

[허전하다] [heojeonhada]

* 1. 주변에 아무것도 없어서 텅 빈 느낌이 있다.

Showing a feeling of emptiness because there is no one around.

* 2. 의지할 곳이 없어지거나 무엇을 잃은 것처럼 서운한 느낌이 있다.

Having a feeling of sadness as if one has lost someone

that one depended on or because something is missing.

* 3. 배 속이 비어서 배가 고픈 느낌이 있다.

Having a feeling of hunger because one's stomach is empty.

허전해

[허전해] [heojeonhae]

허전해요

[허전해요] [heojeonhaeyo]

우리 남편이 떠난 뒤 내 삶에는
큰 빈자리가 생겼어.
After my husband left, there was
a gaping hole in my life.

"허전해"

우리는 오늘 두 아이를 유학 보냈어요.
공항에서 돌아오니 집이 텅 빈 것 같아요.
We sent our two children to study
abroad today. We returned from the
airport to find the house empty.

"허전해요"

라면을 먹는데 김치가 없을 때 드는 마음.
This is how I feel when there's no kimchi
when I eat ramen.

"허전해"

저녁을 안 먹었더니 속이 텅 빈 것 같아.
I didn't have dinner and my stomach
feels empty.

"(속이) 허전해"

결국 모두들 가버리고 나는 혼자 남겨졌어.
Eventually they all drifted away
and I was left alone.

"허전해"

난 요즘 남자친구가 없어서 너무 외로워.
I'm so lonely these days without a boyfriend.

"(옆구리가) 허전해"

우울하다

[우울하다] [uulhada]

* 걱정 등으로 마음이 답답하여 활발한 기운이 없다.

Feeling frustrated and cheerless due to worries, etc.

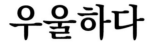

우울해

[우울해] [uulhae]

우울해요

[우울해요] [uulhaeyo]

난 다른 팀원들한테 따돌림당했다고 느껴.
I feel like I've been alienated
by the other team members.
"우울해"

최근에 해고당했고, 크리스마스가 코앞이야.
I got fired recently and
Christmas is just around the corner.
"우울해"

가: 왜 이렇게 우울해? 무슨 일이야?
나: 아무것도 아니야. 그냥 가을 타나 봐.
A: Why are you so blue? What's going on?
B: Nothing. I just get the autumn blues.
"우울해"

내가 하는 일이라곤 밥하고 빨래하고
애들 뒷바라지하는 것뿐인 것 같아.
All I seem to do is cook,
wash and pick up after the kids.
"우울해"

요즘 생각해 보니 그동안 바쁘게 사느라
내 인생에 대해 생각할 시간도 없었어.
뭔가 이루어 놓은 것 없이 나이만 먹는 것 같아.
Thinking about it these days, I haven't had
time to reflect on my life because I've been
busy. I feel like I'm getting older without
accomplishing anything.
"우울해"

허탈하다

[허탈하다] [heotalhada]

* 몸의 기운이 빠지고 정신이 멍하다.
Losing one's energy and becoming absent-minded.

●

허탈해
[허탈해] [heotalhae]

허탈해요
[허탈해요] [heotalhaeyo]

●

투자자가 없어서 내 사업 아이디어가
없던 일이 되었어요.
My business idea went out the window
due to a lack of investors.

"허탈해요"

최근에 20년을 일한 회사에서 정리해고를
당했어.
I was recently made redundant after
20 years in a company.

"허탈해"

경기에 진 선수들은 바닥에 주저앉았어.
The players who lost the game collapsed
to the ground.

"허탈해"

비행기가 결항된 후로 우리 여행 계획은
없던 일이 되었어.
Our travel itinerary went out the window
after the plane was canceled.

"허탈해"

우리가 했던 모든 일들이 실패로 돌아갔어요.
Everything we've done went out the window.

"허탈해요"

열심히 준비했지만 결과가 좋지 못해 실망스러워.
I prepared for this so hard that it's such a
letdown that the results are unfavorable.

"허탈해"

미안하다

[미안하다] [mianhada]

* 남에게 잘못을 하여 마음이 편치 못하고 부끄럽다.

Feeling rather uncomfortable and ashamed because one did something bad to someone.

미안해

[미안해] [mianhae]

미안해요

[미안해요] [mianhaeyo]

이런 말을 너한테 하지 말 걸 그랬어.

널 우울하게 할 생각은 없었어.

I shouldn't have said this to you.

I didn't mean to bring you down.

"미안해"

캐물으려고 한 건 아니에요.

I didn't mean to pry.

"미안해요"

차가 너무 막혀서 10분쯤 늦을 거야.

I'm stuck in traffic and I'll be about

10 minutes late.

"미안해"

어떡하지?

오늘 친구 생일인데 까맣게 잊고 있었어.

What should I do? It's my friend's

birthday today, but I completely forgot.

"미안해"

회사에 무슨 일이 생겨서 오늘 못 갈 것 같아.

Something's come up at work,

and I don't think I can make it tonight.

"미안해"

난 벌써 친구에게 여러 번 부탁을 했었는데,

오늘 또 부탁을 해야 해.

I've already asked my friend many times,

but I have to ask her again today.

"미안해"

슬프다

[슬프다] [seulpeuda]

* 눈물이 날 만큼 마음이 아프고 괴롭다.

Sad and sorrowful enough to make one cry.

●

슬퍼

[슬퍼] [seulpeo]

슬퍼요

[슬퍼요] [seulpeoyo]

●

영화를 보는 내내 울었어.

I cried throughout the movie.

"슬퍼"

내 가장 친한 친구가 해외로 이사를 가.
오늘이 친구와 보내는 마지막 날이라고
생각하니 눈물이 나.

My best friend is moving abroad.
It makes me cry to think that today is
the last day I will spend with my friend.

"슬퍼"

어린 시절부터 나와 함께 자라던 개가 죽었어요.
우린 15년을 함께 했었어요.

My dog, who had been growing up with me
since childhood, died.
We had been together for 15 years.

"슬퍼요"

우리 부모님께서 일찍 돌아가셔서 할머니께서
저를 키워주셨어요.
할머니가 돌아가셨다는 소식을 들었을 때 드는 마음.

My parents died early, so my grandmother
raised me. This is how I felt when I heard that
my grandmother passed away.

"슬퍼요"

내가 가장 아끼는 물건이 이사하는 도중에 없어졌어.

My most cherished item disappeared while
moving.

"슬퍼"

아프다

[아프다] [apeuda]

* 1. 다치거나 병이 생겨 통증이나 괴로움을 느끼다.

Feeling pain or suffering due to an injury or illness.

* 2. 몸의 어떤 부분을 많이 사용해서 피로나 괴로움을 느끼다.

Feeling fatigue or suffering from overuse of a body part.

* 3. 슬픔이나 연민으로 마음에 괴로운 느낌이 있다.

Feeling pain in the heart due to sadness or a lingering attachment.

아파
[아파] [apa]

아파요
[아파요] [apayo]

우리 아들이 아팠을 때 제대로 된 약도
한번 못썼어.
I wasn't able to give my son any proper
medicine when he was sick.
      "(마음이) 아파"

이번 계약 조건은 상당히 복잡해요.
The terms and conditions of this contract
are quite complicated.
      "(머리가) 아파요"

오늘 여행 와서 하루 종일 걸어 다녔어.
그래서 더 이상은 못 걷겠어요.
I came on a trip and walked all day today.
so I can't walk anymore.
      "(다리가) 아파요"

내 친구가 불치병으로 고통스러워한다는 것을
들었어.
I heard the news that my friend is suffering
from an incurable disease.
      "(마음이) 아파요"

날 위해 모든 것을 희생하신 어머니를 생각할 때
드는 마음.
This is how I feel when I think about my
mother who sacrificed everything for me.
      "(마음이) 아파요"

서럽다

[서ː럽따] [seoːreoptta]

* 억울하고 슬프다.
To be sad and depressed.

●

서러워

[서ː러워] [seoːreowo]

서러워요

[서ː러워요] [seoːreowoyo]

●

외국에서 혼자 살아서 아플 때 챙겨줄 사람이
아무도 없어.
I live alone abroad, so there's no one
to take care of me when I'm sick.

"서러워"

이민 와서 최근에 마음고생을 많이 했어요.
After emigrating, I've been through a lot
of heartaches lately.

"서러워요"

늙고 병든 것도 힘든데 자식들한테 구박까지
당하고 있어.
As if it wasn't bad enough to be old and sick,
I am even abused by my children.

"서러워"

배고파 죽겠는데 돈이 없어.
I'm starving to death, but I have no money.

"서러워"

난 열심히 공부했는데 이번 시험이 너무 어려웠어.
그래서 난 좋은 점수를 못 받았어.
내가 속상해하고 있는데 선생님께서 다음 시험공부를
열심히 하라고 충고하셨어.
I studied hard, but this exam was really difficult.
So I didn't get a good grade.
I was upset, but the teacher advised me to study
harder for the next exam.

"서러워"

속상하다

[속ː쌍하다] [sokːssanghada]

* 일이 뜻대로 되지 않아 마음이 편하지 않고 괴롭다.

Feeling discomfort and anguish because things do not go one's way.

●

속상해

[속ː쌍해] [sokːssanghae]

속상해요

[속ː쌍해요] [sokːssanghaeyo]

●

나만 빼놓고 친구들이 쇼핑몰에 갔어.

My friends went to the mall without me.

"속상해"

지난 주말에 새 차를 받았어요.

그런데 오늘 아침에 범퍼가 찌그러졌어요.

I got a new car last weekend.

But I got a dent on my bumper this morning.

"속상해요"

승진하려고 노력했는데 이번에 승진을 못했어요.

I tried to get promoted, but I failed to
achieve it this time.

"속상해요"

집안이 온통 뒤숭숭해서 내 건강이 나아지지 않아.

My health haven't been improved by all the
upset at home.

"속상해"

아픈 아들을 두고 출근하려니 발걸음이 떨어지지
않았어.

I found it hard to go to work when my son
was ill.

"속상해"

오늘 가방을 잃어버렸는데 집에 오자마자
엄마한테 혼났어요.

I lost my bag today, but my mom scolded me
when I got home.

"속상해요"

안쓰럽다

[안쓰럽따] [ansseureoptta]

* 1. 자기보다 어리거나 약한 사람에게 도움을 받고 폐를 끼쳐 미안하고 딱하다.

Feeling uneasy and sorry about getting help from

and imposing on someone who is younger or weaker.

* 2. 다른 사람의 처지나 형편이 딱하고 불쌍하여 마음이 좋지 않다.

Feeling upset because someone's situation

or circumstances are bad and pitiful.

●

안쓰러워

[안쓰러워] [ansseureowo]

안쓰러워요

[안쓰러워요] [ansseureowoyo]

●

우리 아내가 임신 8주째인데 입덧이 심해.
My wife is eight weeks pregnant and
suffering from horrible morning sickness.

"안쓰러워"

우리 누나는 남편을 잃고 힘든 시간을 보내고
있어요.
My sister's been going through a hard time
since she lost her husband.

"안쓰러워요"

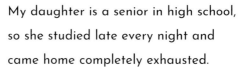

우리 딸은 고3인데 매일 밤늦게까지 공부하고
녹초가 돼서 집에 왔어.
My daughter is a senior in high school,
so she studied late every night and
came home completely exhausted.

"안쓰러워"

내 친구는 공부를 잘해서 충분히 좋은 대학에
갈 수 있어요. 하지만 돈이 없어서 대학가는 걸
포기해야 해요.
My friend can go to a good university
because he's good at studies.
But he has to give up entering a university
because he has no money.

"안쓰러워요"

그의 거친 손은 그가 많은 고생을 했음을 보여줘요.
His rough hands show that he had endured
great hardship.

"안쓰러워요"

불쌍하다

[불쌍하다] [bulssanghada]

* 사정이나 형편이 좋지 않아 가엾고 마음이 슬프다.

Feeling sorry and sad because someone is in a bad situation.

●

불쌍해

[불쌍해] [bulssanghae]

불쌍해요

[불쌍해요] [bulssanghaeyo]

●

추운 겨울날 비를 맞으며 구걸하는 어린아이를
볼 때 드는 마음.
This is how I feel when I see a child begging
in the rain in the cold winter.

"불쌍해요"

갑작스러운 사고로 남편을 잃고 아이와
단둘이 사는 딸을 보면 마음이 아파.
It breaks my heart to see my daughter,
who lost her husband in a sudden accident,
live alone with her child.

"불쌍해"

교통사고로 부모님을 잃은 아이를 보았어.
사고에서 혼자 살아남은 그 아이는 아무것도
모른 채 웃고 있었어.
I saw a child who lost his parents in a traffic
accident. The child who survived the accident
was smiling without knowing anything.

"불쌍해"

많은 동물들이 인터넷을 통해 거래되고 착취 당해.
Many animals are traded and exploited over
the Internet.

"불쌍해"

그 아이들은 태어나자마자 부모에게 버림받았어요.
Those kids were abandoned by their parents
as soon as they were born.

"불쌍해요"

궁금하다

[궁금하다] [gunggeumhada]

* 1. 무엇이 무척 알고 싶다.

Having a strong desire to know about something.

* 2. 무엇이 걱정이 되어 마음이 무척 답답하다.

Feeling heavyhearted worrying about something.

●

궁금해

[궁금해] [gunggeumhae]

궁금해요

[궁금해요] [gunggeumhaeyo]

●

너네들 어떻게 만났어?

How'd you guys meet?

"궁금해"

그곳에 가는 데 얼마나 걸리셨어요?

How long did it take you to get there?

"궁금해요"

기술은 얼마나 더 발전할 수 있을까?

How far can technology advance?

"궁금해"

몸매를 유지하는 비결이 뭐예요?

What's your secret to keeping in shape?

"궁금해요"

내가 걱정하는 건 걔가 일을 잘하고 있는지 야.

What I'm concerned about is whether he's doing his job well.

"궁금해"

이 영화의 예측할 수 없는 결말은 무엇일까?

What will be the unpredictable end of this movie?

"궁금해"

왜 이 차를 산 거야?

Why did you buy this car?

"궁금해"

답답하다

[답따파다] [dapttapada]

* 1. 근심이나 걱정으로 마음이 초조하고 속이 시원하지 않다.

Nervous and uncomfortable due to worry or anxiety.

* 2. 다른 사람의 태도나 상황이 마음에 차지 않아 안타깝다.

Feeling anxious because someone's attitude

or situation is not uncomfortable.

●

답답해

[답따패] [dapttapae]

답답해요

[답따패요] [dapttapaeyo]

●

넌 너무 FM이야. 가끔은 융통성이 있어야지.

You're too by the book.

You need to be flexible sometimes.

"답답해"

내 휴대폰이 고장 나서 지금 아무것도
검색할 수 없어요.

My mobile phone is broken, so I can't
search anything right now.

"답답해요"

더운 여름날 버스를 타고 가던 중 에어컨이
고장 났어요. 공기가 너무 답답하고 땀 냄새가
나요. 버스에서 빨리 내리고 싶어요.

I was on my way by bus on a hot summer
day, but the air conditioner was broken.
The air is so stuffy and smells like sweat.
I can't wait to get off the bus.

"답답해요"

내 남동생은 사소한 일도 쉽게 결정하지
못하고 주저해.

My younger brother hesitates because he
can't decide even the smallest things easily.

"답답해"

걔는 좋다 싫다 말이 없어.

He doesn't say anything one way or the other.

"답답해"

안타깝다

[안타깝따] [antakkaptta]

* 뜻대로 되지 않거나 보기에 가엾고 불쌍해서 가슴이 아프고 답답하다.

Feeling sad and frustrated because something does not work out as planned or someone looks pitiful and pathetic.

●

안타까워
[안타까워] [antakkawo]

안타까워요
[안타까워요] [antakkawoyo]

●

나는 1등으로 달리고 있었는데
결승선 앞에서 넘어졌어.
I was running in the first place,
but I fell in front of the finish line.
"안타까워"

어머니를 여의고 슬픔에 잠겨 있는
남편을 볼 때 드는 마음.
This is how I feel when I see my husband
saddened by the loss of his mother.
"안타까워요"

넌 네가 그렇게까지 사랑했던 여자한테
사랑받지 못했어.
You were never loved back by the girl
you loved so much.
"안타까워"

요즘 할머니의 건강이 급격히 나빠지고 계세요.
My grandmother's health is rapidly
deteriorating nowadays.
"안타까워요"

우린 우리 집이 불길에 휩싸이는 것을
속수무책으로 지켜보았어.
We watched helplessly as our home
went up in flames.
"안타까워"

아쉽다

[아쉽따] [aswiptta]

* 1. 필요한 것이 없거나 모자라서 만족스럽지 못하다.

Unsatisfied because what one needs is missing or deficient.

* 2. 미련이 남아 안타깝고 서운하다.

Sorry and sad due to a lingering attachment.

It means not enough as I want, dissatisfied and regret it.

●

아쉬워
[아쉬워] [aswiwo]

아쉬워요
[아쉬워요] [aswiwoyo]

●

◎ 아쉽다 vs 섭섭하다

· 아쉽다 : 자기 자신으로 인해 실망감이나 미련이 생길 때 사용한다.

When you're disappointed or have regrets because of yourself.

· 섭섭하다 : 타인으로 인해 실망스러울 때 사용한다.

When you're disappointed by someone else.

나 할 일이 너무 많아서 파티에 못 가.

I have a lot of work to do,

so I can't make it to the party.

"아쉬워"

조금만 더 시간이 있었다면 문제를 해결할 수 있었을 텐데.

I could have solved the problem if I had a little more time.

"아쉬워요"

내가 봐 두었던 옷이 오늘부터 할인을 하는데 돈이 없어서 살 수가 없어요.

The clothes I had kept my eyes on are on sale from today, but I can't buy them because I don't have money.

"아쉬워요"

오랜만에 친구들과 만났는데 내일 중요한 회의가 있어서 일찍 가봐야 해요.

I met my friends after a long time, but I have an important meeting tomorrow, so I have to go home early.

"아쉬워요"

오늘 그 식당 문 닫았나 봐. 내가 몇 번이나 전화 걸었는데 안 받네. 여기 꼭 가보고 싶었는데!

I think the restaurant is closed today.

I called several times, but they don't answer.

I really wanted to try this one out!

"아쉬워"

섭섭하다

[섭써파다] [seopsseopada]

* 1. 서운하고 아쉽다.

Sorry and feeling the lack of someone or something.

* 2. 없어지는 것이 슬프고 아깝다.

Sad and sorry about someone or something disappearing.

* 3. 기대에 어긋나 서운하거나 불만스럽다.

Sorry and dissatisfied because something fails to meet one's expectations.

섭섭해

[섭써패] [seopsseopae]

섭섭해요

[섭써패요] [seopsseopaeyo]

◎섭섭하다 vs 서운하다

· 섭섭하다 (서운하다+아쉽다+속상하다): 타인으로 인해 실망스러운데 속상함이 더 클 때 사용한다.

This is used when you're disappointed by others but you're more upset than disappointed.

· 서운하다(안타깝다 +아쉽다 + 그립다) : 타인으로 인해 실망스러운데 그리움이 더 클 때 사용한다.

This is used when you're disappointed by others but you miss them more than being disappointed.

지난주에 친구가 내 결혼식에 못 올 것
같다고 말했어요.

Last week, my friend said, "I don't think
I can make it to your wedding."

"섭섭해요"

내가 일부러 그런 게 아니야.

그런데 우리 남편은 내 마음을 몰라줘.

I didn't do it on purpose.

But my husband doesn't know how I feel.

"섭섭해"

요즘 아들이 사춘기인지 너무 냉정하게 말해.

I'm not sure whether it's because my son
is in puberty these days, but he talks to
me in a very cold manner.

"섭섭해"

걔는 1년 전에 떠난 이후로 나한테 연락 한 번
안 했어요.

She hasn't even contacted me once since
she left a year ago.

"섭섭해요"

가: 이건 우리가 질 수 없는 게임이었어.

나: 내 탓으로 돌리려는 거야?

A: It was a game we could not afford to lose.

B: Are you trying to blame this on me?

"섭섭해"

서운하다

[서운하다] [seounhada]

* 생각처럼 되지 않아 만족스럽지 못하다.

Not satisfied with something because it did not
go according to one's expectation.

●

서운해

[서운해] [seounhae]

서운해요

[서운해요] [seounhaeyo]

●

◎섭섭하다 vs 서운하다

· 섭섭하다 (서운하다+아쉽다+속상하다): 타인으로 인해 실망스러운데 속상함
이 더 클 때 사용한다.

This is used when you're disappointed by others but you're more upset
than disappointed.

· 서운하다(안타깝다 +아쉽다 + 그립다) : 타인으로 인해 실망스러운데 그리움
이 더 클 때 사용한다.

This is used when you're disappointed by others but you miss them more
than being disappointed.

난 걔랑 친하다고 생각했는데 걔 생일파티에
초대받지 못했어.
I thought I was close to her, but I wasn't
invited to her birthday party.

"서운해"

K-pop 그룹의 리더가 그룹을 탈퇴하고 한국을
떠났어.
A K-pop group leader has quit the group
and left South Korea.

"서운해"

오랫동안 사랑받아온 드라마가 끝났어요.
The long-loved drama has reached its end.

"서운해요"

이거 내가 제일 좋아하는 과자인데 단종됐어요.
It's my favorite snack, but it has been
discontinued.

"서운해요"

내가 조금 불평했다고 나한테 그렇게 짜증 낼
필요는 없잖아?
You don't have to be that annoyed with
me just because I complained a bit to you,
do you?

"서운해"

한

[한ː] [hanː]

* 몹시 원망스럽고 억울하거나 안타깝고 슬퍼서 응어리진 마음.
A feeling of bitterness, deep resentment or sorrow that
builds up in one's mind from an unfair or regretful event.

한이다
[한ː이다] [hanːida]

한이 맺혀
[한ː이 매처] [hanːi maecheo]

한이에요
[한ː이에요] [hanːieyo]

한이 맺혀요
[한ː이 매처요] [hanːi maecheoyo]

◎ 맺히다 [매치다] [maechida]

* 좋지 않은 감정이 마음에 남다. For negative feelings to remain in mind.

◎ 한(恨)

한(恨)이라는 것은 순간적인 감정이 아니라 분노, 아쉬움, 안타까움, 또는 이들
모두가 한데 뒤섞인 오래된 감정이다.

한(恨) is not a momentary emotion, but an old emotion in which anger,
regret, painfulness, or all of them are mixed together.

난 평생 억울한 일을 많이 겪었고 원망을 품고 살았어.

I suffered a lot of unfair things and lived with resentment all my life.

"한이 맺혀"

난 어렸을 때 가난해서 학교를 다닐 수 없었어. 그래서 평생 동안 가슴에 담고 살았어.

I was poor when I was little and couldn't go to school.

So I kept it in my mind for the rest of my life.

"(배우지 못한 것이) 한이다"

어렸을 때부터 오랫동안 영어 공부에 어려움을 겪었어. 하지만 마흔이 넘은 지금도 영어에 자신이 없고 잘하지도 못해요.

I have struggled with studying English for a long time since I was little. But I'm still not confident in English nor good at it even now at the age of 40.

"(영어를 못하는 것이) 한이에요"

나는 오랫동안 시댁 식구들에게 불공평한 대우를 받고 차별을 받아 왔어요.

I've been treated unfairly and discriminated against by my in-laws for a long time.

"한이 맺혀요"

시원섭섭하다

[시원섭써파다] [siwonseopsseopada]

* 한편으로는 후련하고 다른 한편으로는 서운하고 아쉽다.
Feeling relieved on the one hand, but feeling sad
and sorry on the other.

●

시원섭섭해

[시원섭써패] [siwonseopsseopae]

시원섭섭해요

[시원섭써패요] [siwonseopsseopaeyo]

●

오늘 우리 딸의 결혼식 날이야. 우리 딸이 좋은 사람을 만나서 너무 행복한데 조금 슬프기도 해.
Today is my daughter's wedding day. I'm very happy that my daughter met the right person, but I'm also a little sad.

"시원섭섭해"

난 낡고 작은 집에 살다가 10년 만에 새 집을 샀어. 마침내, 이사하는 날 아침, 오래된 집에서 살았을 때 즐겁고 행복했던 기억이 떠올랐어.
I lived in an old and small house but bought a new house after 10 years. Finally, on the morning I moved in, I remembered the pleasant and happy memories of living in an old house.

"시원섭섭해"

더 좋은 회사로 이직하게 되어 오늘 마지막으로 근무하는 날이에요. 때때로 힘든 일도 있었지만 동료들과 함께 즐겁게 일하던 날들이 기억나요.
I ended up moving to a better company, so today is my last work day. Despite the strenuous matters at times, I remember the days of enjoying working with my colleagues.

"시원섭섭해요"

책을 쓰느라 힘들었어요. 하지만 책을 다 쓰고 나니 마음이 놓이기도 하고 슬프기도 해요.
I had a hard time writing a book. But now that I've finished it, I feel both relieved and sad.

"시원섭섭해요"